A REMEMBERED LAND

Recollections of Life in the Countryside
1880–1914
Edited by Sean Street

A Country Diary Book

Michael Joseph
London

Also by Sean Street

Prose
A Hampshire Miscellany
Tales of Old Dorset
The Wreck of the Deutschland: an Historical
   Note
Petersfield: a Pictorial Past
The Wreck of the Deutschland
The Bournemouth Symphony Orchestra: A
   Centenary Celebration (*with Ray Carpenter*)
The Dymock Poets

Plays
A Shepherd's Life
Wessex Days
Tea Set and Match
Honest John
Mathias

Musical Works (*with Douglas Coombes*)
The Treasure Trail
The Benjamin Dream
Papa Panov's Special Christmas
Young Copperfield
The Winter Bird

Poetry
Earth and Sky
Figure in a Landscape
Carvings
A Walk in Winter
This True Making

MICHAEL JOSEPH LTD
Published by the Penguin Group
27 Wrights Land, London W8 5TZ
Viking Penguin Inc., 375 Hudson Street, New York, New York 10014, USA
Penguin Books Australia Ltd, Ringwood, Victoria, Australia
Penguin Books Canada Ltd, 10 Alcorn Avenue, Toronto, Ontario, Canada M4V 3B2
Penguin Books (NZ) Ltd, 182–190 Wairau Road, Auckland 10, New Zealand

Penguin Books Ltd, Registered Offices: Harmondsworth, Middlesex, England

First published in Great Britain 1994

Filmset by Selwood Systems, Midsomer Norton
Printed in Great Britain by
Butler & Tanner Ltd, Frome and London

ISBN 0 7181 3829 5

The moral right of the editor has been asserted

CONTENTS

The sounds of England, the tinkle of the hammer on the anvil in the country smithy, the corncrake on a dewy morning, the sound of the scythe against the whetstone, and the sight of a plough team coming over the brow of a hill, the sight that has been seen in England since England was a land, and may be seen in England long after the Empire has perished and every works in England has ceased to function, for centuries the one eternal sight of England. The wild anemones in the woods in April, the last load at night of hay being drawn down a lane as the twilight comes on, when you can scarcely distinguish the figures of the horses as they take it home to the farm, and above all, most subtle, most penetrating and most moving, the smell of wood smoke coming up in an autumn evening, or the smell of the scutch fires: that wood smoke that our ancestors, tens of thousands of years ago, must have caught on the air when they were coming home with the result of the day's forage when they were still nomads, and when they were still roaming the forests and the plains of the continent of Europe. These things strike down into the very depths of our nature, and touch chords that go back to the beginning of time and the human race, but they are chords that with every year of our life sound a deeper note in our innermost being. These are the things that make England, and I grieve for it that they are not the childish inheritance of the majority of the people today in our country.

Stanley Baldwin, *On England*

INTRODUCTION

The late nineteenth and early twentieth century was a period of accelerating change in the British countryside – change that was to reach its climax with the start of the First World War. For centuries, life in the fields and villages of Britain had gone on largely unaltered. Certainly it is true that during the nineteenth century there had been occasionally violent protests at the introduction of farm machines, and a rising sense of injustice at some of the low wages that were paid to workers, but in 1840, when Thomas Hardy was born at Bockhampton in Dorset, country living was very much what it had always been: a blending of the human and natural worlds that reflected the ebb and flow inherent in the rhythm of the seasons.

Throughout the nineteenth century, there had been a gradual but inexorable shift of cultural emphasis away from the countryside towards the towns and cities. Now, from about 1880, things began to move faster – literally. The first electric trains in Britain started operating – in Portrush, Northern Ireland and Brighton – in 1883, part of the continuing revolution in mobility brought about by the arrival of the railways. With the growth of industry there was an increasing movement of workers from the country to the cities, leading often to poverty and squalid conditions for thousands who could not make the urban dream come true. In 1891 it became possible for a London telephone subscriber to make a telephone call to Paris, only a year after the same caller was first able to ring a number in Birmingham. Three years later the Manchester Ship Canal was completed, and by 1895 the use of gas instead of oil as a source of fuel for lighting, cooking and heating was spreading throughout the country. In the same year, the National Trust was founded, based on the fear that the spread of industry and growing population would wipe out some of the finest countryside and architecture.

1914 was in some ways also a culmination of a process that had been accelerating for years. It was the consciousness that significant change was in the air regarding man's relationship with the countryside that led to the wealth of rural writing and recollection that came into being during – and after – the period. Those of us who did not live through them may look back on those years as a sort of casting-out from Eden; what is interesting is that so many people who *were* part of the time also remembered rural life in late Victorian and Edwardian Britain with regret at the passing of a way of life in which men and women were somehow more at one with the world in which they lived.

This book is an attempt to capture the essence of rural Britain during those years when it became clear that long-term profound change was inevitable. That essence is seen through the eyes of those who recalled the unadorned truth of them. In their writing there is nostalgia of course, but there is also an affection for the land and rural life that is realistic. Times and life could be very hard, but most of the writers who were there remembered a way of living that was good enough to mourn in its passing.

There was, between 1880 and 1914, a wealth of professional writing on the countryside, much of it work that would become cherished as literature. Richard Jefferies, W. H. Hudson and Edward Thomas form a peak of country writing which deserves to be read far more today than it actually is. You will find them among these pages. In making this selection I have also sought to explore some of the less well-known authors of the time. Among these, one of the most gratifying discoveries has been the Berkshire author, Eleanor G. Hayden. She was a chronicler of the countryside who impressed Edward Thomas, himself an astute and respected literary critic.

Edith Holden, whose words and illustrations are present in each chapter of this book, wrote the book that became famous as *The Country Diary of an Edwardian Lady* in 1906. She represents a vast body of work by observers of the rural world, some of whom are read very little, if at all, today. And so, around the strong professional voices, I have placed some of the many little-known accounts of the men and women for whom the rural world was not a place into which they escaped, but a practical world upon which they relied for their livelihood and their way of life. This murmur of voices tells us of a place of ancient tradition, of folklore, of the social structure within the tiniest community and of the ever-present partnership between the natural world and the weather. They were part of an oral heritage that no longer exists, and the images and memories they have left us are all the more precious because they are irreplaceable.

The concern of writers was matched by the photographers of the time, and whose photographs here reflect how the still-young miracle of the camera captured the images of the passing age. Although there was no colour photography as we know it today, the picture-tinter's skill left us with a rural world reflected in subtle and gentle pastels, enhancing the golden glow with which the imagination bathes a time of passing innocence before the first great catastrophe of the twentieth century.

Occasionally the storytellers have drawn me back further into the rural past; after all, the venerable countryman, telling his tale in the 1880s, would have had grandparents who were alive as far back as the middle of the eighteenth century. This overlapping of generations brings us close to a world we had thought once to be so far away. For the most part, though, it is the sunset of the rural tradition that is commemorated in this book. We owe those who have preserved that way of life a great debt of gratitude. What they have left us is a part of our history. It teaches us something vital to take with us as we move towards the twenty-first century. It is the echo of a way of life that once must have seemed as if it would never disappear. It is above all, the voice of human experience. It is indeed a thing to celebrate.

Note. Where a region is not apparent from the quotation or the source, a county name is given (if known).

LANDSCAPE
AND
THE NATURAL
WORLD

Sept. 12th. Drove to Dartsmeet from Princetown. Gorgeous colouring everywhere. Parts of the high-lying moorland are white with short bleached grasses contrasting strongly with the dark patches of purple heather and gold of the gorse. The valley below the meeting of the East and West Darts was a perfect picture.

Edith Holden, *The Nature Notes of an Edwardian Lady*

The diverse landscape of Britain has three major essences: as a terrain of changing, often breathtaking beauty, as a practical place of work, and as home for a unique diversity of flora and fauna. There has long been the view of the countryside as being a haven into which the townsperson can escape, while at the same time being a sort of factory in which workers saw the shape of a field or the contours of a down as being appropriate or otherwise to the tasks of a countryman. The practical view did not mean that the country dweller was blind to the beauty around him or her – far from it: it was more that the rural populace grew through generations in the same landscape, as though they were a part of it themselves.

And it was an intimacy which led to a deep understanding of the flowers, plants and wild creatures with which they shared their world. But if we seek the detail in that landscape we, like the countryman, must stop and stare, move closer, examine and study the specifics of the natural world of which it is composed. As the village dweller of 1880 to 1914 had an unsentimental attitude to landscape and animals, so was his view of the natural world equally practical. It was not a self-conscious noting-down of bird song or of certain flowers: these things were ever-present in an age when there seemed no cause to fear that they might one day cease to exist. Today, many of those tiny worlds that were a part of life for our ancestors in their landscape are lost to us for ever.

WHAT A PARADISE is England, infinite in variety, cloistered in calm and quiet ... The little fields are edged with thorns and briars that create the garden of England as they destroyed the garden of Eden. The dark and lonesome terrors of the old forests that once smothered the surface are transformed into spinneys and woods, where dappled light and shade draw sweet-singing birds from the distant south and make homes for flowers as sweet in scent as in hue. Thus today the floor of the ousted forest surpasses the most precious garden ... The humble houses, often built of stone and straw and wood and brick got from the neighbouring land, seem to have grown straight out from the soil; and harbour communities still as true to the spirit of the place as a river to its bed.

Sir William Beach Thomas, *The Way of a Countryman*
Cumbria

THE ENGLAND OF my dreams is of a magical nature. It appears to me as a green chalk hill, high and strong, running towards the sunset. Far behind you, as you walk westward, lie the smoke and wealth of herded men – who are English, too, but do

not live in my dream-country. In the bottoms that run north and south into the long ridge are secret and friendly villages, the homes of those who have made the earth rich by their secular labour. The hill ends in a little forsaken port, where change comes not, nor does any man grow old.

That England is built up partly from my intimate love of one place, Bridport Harbour in Dorset, where the world for me seems to end, and partly from many walks I have taken on the Dorset hills on my way to that haven of rest. Once in particular I seemed to be really in that England of my fantasy. I stood with a companion in great contentment on a great hill, looking out over the blue and golden mists where Bridport lay against the dazzling sea. The earth stretched away into infinite sunshine, and I felt as if I were contemplating the ultimate peace on earth for which the ages have striven, and were part of it, able to continue in it for ever. Yet as I turned away I knew I must soon go back to less happy places, must face menacing hopes and fears, perform tasks, live and die; not dream.

F. J. Harvey Darton, *The Marches of Wessex*

BEYOND REETH, SWALEDALE becomes a country to be explored with some determination and courage . . . Here one is really out of the world. Railways seem to be a thousand miles away, and one is apt to forget that the telegraph wire has found its way into these solitudes – lingering here, indeed, one has no wish to know that the way has been found. It is true that, after all, one is not so far from the swift means of returning to any point of the compass – it is only five miles over the hills

to Redmire in Wensleydale, and only ten back to Richmond. But looking about one at the hillsides, pitted with the scars from whence human hands have dug forth lead for at least two thousand years, and at the valleys, fading away amongst the mountains, and apparently devoid of all but the scantiest evidences of human life, one can easily, with the aid of a little imagination, believe that one has come into a solitude which nothing ever has disturbed and nothing can ever transform.

J. S. Fletcher, The Enchanting North
North Yorkshire

BY CLEEVE MILL, where clouds of sweet-smelling flour issued from the doorway, we disembarked and climbed up between the thorn trees until upon the ridge we could look back upon the green vale of Evesham, and southward across ploughed fields, and cottages among orchards and elms, to the grey line of the Cotswolds, over

which a patch of silver hung, as the day fought hard to regain its morning sunshine
. . . We paused on the brow of the slope above Avon for a longer look. At our feet
was spread the vale of Evesham; the river, bordered with meadows as green and flat
as billiard-tables; the stream of Arrow to northward, which rises in the Lickey hills,
and comes down through Alcester to join the Avon here; the villages of Salford
Priors and Salford Abbots; farther to the west, among its apple trees, the roofs and
gables of Salford Nunnery, the village of Harvington. And all down the stream, and
round the meadows, and in and out of these

low farms,
Poor pelting villages, sheepcotes, and mills,

are willows innumerable – some polled last year, and looking like green mops, others
with long curved branches ready to be lopped and turned into fence poles next
winter, until they are lost in the hills round Evesham, where the dim towers stand
up and the bold outline of Bredon Hill shuts out the view of the Severn Valley.

Sir Arthur Quiller-Couch, *The Warwickshire Avon*

IT IS A PLEASANT walk on a fine day, in any season, to Staining. For after you leave
Newton Drive – on the left are fields, part of Layton Hawes, two thousand acres of
'common land' once extending halfway to what is now St Annes, belonging to the
people and 'enclosed' (plain English, 'stolen') by Act of Parliament in the eighteenth
century, when so much common land was 'annexed' by the landed proprietors; and
on the right the green upland on the crest of which is Whinney Heys Farm . . . you
are in a pretty typical Windmill Land or Fylde lane; not the most beautiful sample
of a Fylde lane, I admit; you must get farther afield for the fairest; but still one
possessing the happy Fylde characteristics of green joy and azure benediction, and,
above all, that delectably soothing magic, which you find nowhere else (anyhow, I
don't), that emparadies the heart with restfulness and blesses the soul with peace.
Because of this holy healing spell I call it the Felicitous Fylde. Not the Sublime
Fylde, nor the Grand Fylde, for there is no wondrous wild nor romantic scenery, but
the Felicitous Fylde, because it fills one with a quiet celestial feeling that mighty
mountains with gorges and torrents, souvenirs of the violent volcanic epochs when
the earth's crust was subject to tremendous and dreadful fiery agitations and
earthquake disturbances, can never give. For all scenery retains more or less the

character of its origin, and though the great mountains are now as still as statues, they mysteriously impress the soul of the beholder with vague thoughts and wonders of the turmoil in which they had birth, while such level pastoral plains as the Fylde, this Windmill Land, the gentle result of ages of sedimentary deposit, enchant the heart with the deliciously drowsing lullaby of musical waters and the droning murmur of tender tides.

Allen Clarke, *Windmill Land*
Lancashire

LEAVING WHITFIELD WE ascended the vale by the quite excellent road that crosses the wild moors to Alston, some nine miles distant. It was an afternoon that will abide in my memory, for the complete and impressive solitude of nearly the whole route, and also for the fact that the road climbs steadily uphill without wavering for a moment, to the fifth milestone, to commence, almost immediately, a similar descent on the Cumbrian side. One of the loftiest and loneliest road passes in England is this, without a doubt. As we breasted the long hill from Whitfield the sunshine vanished, and gloomy clouds, though as yet sailing high, took possession of the sky and drove away the radiance that had hitherto lit up the hills and cast shadows over the vales. Our road crawled slowly up the long steep above the green but treeless glen below, in whose hollow we could see the bright streams of the West Allen rippling down from farm to farm till the last small modest homestead, with its stone wall enclosures, gave way to the wild. Long before we had touched the watershed we, too, were out on the heather among the uneasy grouse, and the intermittent bleat of Cheviot and blackfaced sheep ... Elsewhere beneath the dull and now thickening clouds and the approach of evening, this expanse of primitive upland, which broke away to the south and east into rounded and cone-shaped heights, breathed feelingly in the breeze that whistled in the rushes of the spirit of solitude. We were virtually in the Pennine range, for the moors around us rolled onward till they climbed the heights of Cross Fell, and looked right down upon the Lake country. As we topped the watershed, and began after no long time to dip westward, a quite striking downward view of the hill-girdled hollow, where Alston lay upon the infant streams of the South Tyne, was unfolded.

A. G. Bradley, *The Romance of Northumberland*

THERE IS ALWAYS the sky, there are always the clouds and the sense of plentiful breathing-room above and around the country town. As you perceive, the shops and dwelling-houses are but a thin screen, a flimsy and often beautiful scene-painting hiding the open country but not really shutting it out ... From out there behind the houses and across the valleys comes a fancy of coppices full of primroses, hangers fringed with catkins, woodland hollows still open to the April sky, but soon to be curtained in with young leaves. There were never lovelier hedgerows, deeper meadows, more ample downs, or farms more peaceful, than those one is tempted to imagine from the High Street of a country town.

George Sturt, *Memoirs of a Surrey Labourer*

HOW I LOVE the shadows on the hills! The Vale holds up no such clear mirror wherein to trace the swift passage of the clouds, though one may sometimes watch them scudding across the warm brown earth of a field lying fallow. Yet here, too, kind Mother Nature makes the balance even. Never until I left the downland did I learn how beautiful is the shadow which a forest tree will cast over a field of ripening corn. Once marked, the sight yields continually increasing pleasure.

Other compensations there are for the loss of the delicate play of light and shade on the downs. The changes in the face of heaven, which formerly I saw dimly from above, I now see close at hand. From the moorland road one can follow the course of the storms as they sweep down from the ridge, blot out the distance and bring the horizon within reach of one's hand, passing onward to leave the sun shining through the ragged fringes of the thunder-cloud. Or one can watch far off beyond the flats, where the river valley winds and church spires gleam white against the sullen north, the double rainbow slowly climb the steep sides of the purple mountain masses in the sky, and stretch 'its giant span into infinity'.

In this low-lying tract the mists hang heavily, and on such a fragrant evening . . . the hedgeless fields are not infrequently seamed with broad bands of vapour. The effect they produce, resting soft, snow-white and cloudy, between the rich green of the plain below and the gorgeous hues of the sunset above, is singularly picturesque.

Eleanor G. Hayden, *Islands in the Vale*
Berkshire

A HAZE LIES about the Downs and softens their smooth outline as in summer, if you can but face the bleak wind which never rests up there. The outline starts on the left hand fairly distinguished against the sky. As it sweeps round, it sings, and is lost in the bluish haze; gradually it rises again, and is visible on the right, where the woods stand leafless on the ridge. Or the vapour settles down thicker, and the vast expanse becomes gloomy in broad day. The formless hills loom round about, the roads and marks of civilization seem blotted out, it may be some absolute desert for aught that appears. An immense hollow filled with mist lies underneath. Presently the wind drifts the earth-cloud along, and there by a dark copse are three or four horsemen eagerly seeking a way through the plantation. They are two miles distant, but as plainly visible as if you could touch them. By-and-by one finds a path, and in a single file the troop rides into the wood. On the other side there is a long stretch of open ploughed field, and about the middle of it little white dots close together, sweeping along as if the wind drove them. Horsemen are galloping on the turf at the edge of the arable, which is doubtless heavy going. The troop that has worked through the wood labours hard to overtake; the vapour follows again, and horsemen and hounds are lost in the abyss.

Richard Jefferies, *The Life of the Fields*
Sussex

To a Wiltshire man Salisbury Plain *is* Wiltshire, the very centre of that county – sometimes very bleak, often pretty bare, but there it is with its great chalky, central heart; its most ancient of all prehistoric temples or monumental remains, such as Avebury and Stonehenge; whilst there below its southern spurs may now and then be seen an occasional glimpse of that magnificent example of the stone-craftsman's art – Salisbury Cathedral with its artistic, tapering spire rising from the valley, absolutely refusing to be submerged or deleted from a picture, the like of which cannot perhaps be equalled in this England of ours . . .

S. G. Kendall, *Farming Memoirs of a West Country Yeoman*

By Kenley, Hughley, Easthope and Brockton, we went over two edges that were edges indeed, and sharp edge up. It was impossible to ride up, and dangerous to ride down. Along the top of Wenlock Edge there is one of the most beautiful roads in the kingdom for scenery for many miles. Right and left are grand views over a country rich and fertile – primitive enough, yet teeming with tradition, history and ancient halls.

Fletcher Moss, *Pilgrimages to Old Homes*
Shropshire

ABOVE THE MILL, to the north, the land rises in long, lustrous, melodiously swelling lawns of perfect green to the dark borders of a beech wood, where the sweet, thick air fills the hollows among the virginal foliage with blue. In one place the beeches have parted and made a broad avenue for the eye to travel towards a noble stone house, many-angled, many-windowed, grey, discreet, holding, or on such a day seeming to h   uman life worthy to walk upon the long lawns to the mill, where now nothi   ves except the divine sunlight and, in the hollows, its little cloudy elves.

Edward Thomas, *The Heart of England*

THE VIEW FROM the Abbey terrace is across a vast, verdant, undulating valley of the richest pasture land – a plain without a level stretch in it. It ever rolls away into shallow valley and low hill, with now and then a wooded height or the glittering track of a stream. The land is broken up into a thousand fields, fringed by luxuriant hedges. In every hedge are many trees; trees follow every buff-coloured road, and gather around every hamlet or cluster of farm buildings. It is a country of dairies. Everywhere are there cows, for the smell of cows is the incense of North Dorset.

Sir Frederick Treves, *Highways and Byways in Dorset*

OUR PICTURESQUE OLD orchard was clinging to one side of a romantic ravine, which suddenly, in those days, opened up a vista of exquisite beauty at the bottom of a hill, especially if seen from the opposite side of the vale when the apple trees were in their fullest bloom. This orchard ran up towards a natural combe, and for some distance on the hillside the steep bank on one side of the ravine was planted with not only rare and choice fruit, but also varieties for producing an excellent blend of cider; but the remains of that orchard today, like the writer of these memoirs, have now grown old; and many years since, this picturesque vale has been spoilt by comparison with its once well-kept natural beauty, by the raids of the prospective

builder, although the combe at the head of the orchard may still have retained some small measure of its original dignity.

S. G. Kendall, *Farming Memoirs of a West Country Yeoman*
Wiltshire

THE WHITEWATER ESTUARY stretches far and wide beyond the meadow, and at times of the year like the present, when 'longen folk to gon on pilgrimages', I am filled with a keen desire to travel. Not to go abroad, not to journey to some sun-stricken town in a far-off land where the civilization we know best is not, but to cross the shining estuary and explore the villages on the far side of the river. I have travelled, have been north and south and east and to the isles of the sea; certain far lands and wild peoples are no longer strange to me, but the mysterious country across the estuary enshrines more possibilities than Tibet. The sun lights up tiny villages set amid prosperous fields, a telescope brings them seemingly within reach, but I am no nearer. Villagers who have passed more than eighty years on this side of the Whitewater have never been across the estuary . . .

S. L. Bensusan, *A Countryside Chronicle*
Essex

THE ROMANS BUILT roads 'as straight as a ramrod', as they used to say when ramrods were in regular use in country houses in the days of muzzle-loading guns. Though I never saw a muzzle-loader used, one stood in the corner of the dairy and the beautifully embossed copper powder flask hung from a nail against the fireplace on the wall of the dining-room. There were the remains of a Roman road on the downs and parts of several of the 'turnpike' roads were said to have been of Roman make originally. It was said almost as if it was an apology for their straightness; for no countryman seemed to like a long stretch of straight road. The distance seems longer when one can look down a road for nearly a mile and such a road is often very monotonous.

H. S. Joyce, *I Was Born in the Country*

THE AIR WAS wine, the moist earth-smell wine, the lark's song, the wafts from the cowshed at the top of the field, the pant and smoke of a distant train – all were wine – or song, was it? or odour, this unity they all blent into? I had no words then to describe it, that earth-effluence of which I was so conscious; nor, indeed have I found words since. I ran sideways, shouting; I dug glad heels into the squelching soil; I splashed diamond showers from puddles with a stick; I hurled clods skywards at random, and presently I somehow found myself singing. The words were mere nonsense – irresponsible babble; the tune was an improvisation, a weary, unrhythmic thing of rise and fall: and yet it seemed to me a genuine utterance, and just at that moment the one thing fitting and right and perfect. Humanity would have rejected it with scorn. Nature, everywhere singing in the same key, recognized and accepted it without a flicker of dissent.

Kenneth Grahame, *The Golden Age*

LAST NIGHT I thought the nightingales had come: this corner of the county is very dear to them. I was wrong. The song came from a late blackbird uttering a succession of low flute-like notes after the rest of the birds had gone to sleep . . .

S. L. Bensusan, *A Countryside Chronicle*
Essex

23 JULY 1904: After dinner Boys and Baines went on the River, & 23rd Mother and I went to see Miss Northcroft off, & to buy a boat hook. Then we went to Worcester to feed the swans, we found some, & some cygnets. The cygnets were grey, with almost grey beaks & feet; some of them had feather sheaths still on their young feathers. The swans & ducks fed out of our hands, & one swan bit a hole in my thumb. Some boys were fishing close by, & the fish came for the bread which we gave the swans. We had gooseberries & sponge cake for tea which we had under a horse chestnut tree. We saw a Thrush which was hitting a snailshell against the parth, so as to get the snail out, and eat it . . . We saw a lot of Arrowhead, & flowering-Rush & goldenrod & lithram & Epilobiun & Water Lilies, yellow and white, & creeping-jenny, & tansy in flower. We had dinner in a fairly netly field, & afterwards Boy bathed, with a fairly good effect. Then we paddled, & got plenty of Plantorbises; they are like flat snail-shells. Then we went home.

The childhood diary of Naomi Mitchison, *As It Was*

IT WAS ON AN April day, when the gorse on the Herringfleet Hills was in full blaze of bloom, that I sailed down the Waveney to St Olave's Bridge, and moored for the night just above the old Bell Inn. The day had been warm and cloudless – almost like a fine day at the end of May – and the night was so warm that at midnight I opened my cabin window and lay in my bunk for an hour, looking out over the river. The moon had risen above the hills, and the old inn, the brush-topped willows, the cottages on the shore, and the masts of the wherries on the river, were clearly outlined, like Indian ink silhouettes, against a sky-background of star-speckled, slaty blue, while a shimmering lane of silvery light stretched from the cabin window to the dark shore. Not a breath of wind stirred the dark-plumed reeds and slender willow wands, but across the sky drifted little pearly clouds and films of mist. The curved white ironwork of the bridge – beneath which the tide was ebbing – gleamed in the moonlight like a lunar rainbow.

William A. Dutt, *The Norfolk Broads*

MY CHILDHOOD IN Tonypandy took a turn for the better when my eldest sister Ada May married a young farmer bailiff, who worked on Palla Farm, St Brides in the Vale of Glamorgan. It is impossible to put into words the excitement that our visits to Palla Farm brought to me. I remember one night when we were walking home from a chapel concert along unlit roads: seeing a light like a torch in the hedge. I called out in excitement and asked Ada May to look at it. In the superior, if not patronizing, tone that some country dwellers reserve for 'townies', she said: 'Oh, it's only a glow worm.' If only she knew: it was the only glow worm that I have seen in my long life.

George Thomas, Viscount Tonypandy, *Country Living*

ONCE AT THE summit under the beeches, and there a comfortable seat may be found upon the moss. The wood stretches away beneath for more than a mile in breadth, and beyond it winds the narrow mere glittering in the rays of the early spring sunshine. The bloom is on the blackthorn, but not yet on the may; the hedges are but just awakening from their long winter sleep, and the trees have hardly put forth a sign. But the rooks are busily engaged in the trees of the park, and away yonder at the distant colony in the elms of the meadows. The wood is restless with life . . .

Richard Jefferies, *The Gamekeeper at Home*
Sussex

HOW OFTEN HAVE I laid on the heather listening to the curlew at nesting time . . . calling . . . calling – with no other sound but the soft rustle of the heathland grasses or the occasional bark of a raven flying overhead. The flute-like call of the ring-ouzel ('ouzlem bird' the old village folk called it), the 'clack clack' of the wheatears on Sussex downland was my country music, with the full orchestra playing in the dawn chorus and only the voice of the farmer calling in the cows for the morning milking.

Reg Gammon, *One Man's Furrow*
Hampshire

THE GRASS IN the meadow or home-field as it begins to grow tall in spring is soon visited by the corncrakes, who take up their residence there. In this district (though called the corncrake) these birds seem to frequent the mowing-grass more than the arable fields, and they generally arrive about the time when it has grown sufficiently high and thick to hide their motions. This desire of concealment – to be out of sight – is apparently more strongly marked in them than in any other bird; yet they utter their loud call of 'Crake, crake, crake!' not unlike the turning of a wooden rattle, continuously though only at a short distance.

It is difficult to tell from what place the cry proceeds: at one moment it sounds almost close at hand, the next fifty yards off; then, after a brief silence, a long way to one side or the other. The attempt to mark the spot is in vain; you think you have it, and rush there, but nothing is to be seen, and minutes afterwards 'Crake, crake!' comes behind you.

Richard Jefferies, *Wild Life in a Southern County*
Wiltshire

IN MOST COUNTIES the bee is considered as a peculiarly apt subject of augury for good or ill. In Dorsetshire it is believed that if a humble-bee (dumble-dore) comes inside the house it denotes the arrival of a stranger during the day. You must not, however, drive it out or it will bring you ill luck, for such an act is looked upon as driving out a friend . . . The time of year at which the swarming should take place in order to be of value to the owner is shown by the following lines:

A swarm of bees in May
Is worth a load of hay.
A swarm of bees in June
Is worth a silver spoon.
A swarm of bees in July
Is not worth a fly.

John Symonds Udal, *Dorsetshire Folk-Lore*

WHEN I LIVED at Aldeburgh, I used to lie awake at night listening to the curlews flying over the village. They seemed to have a route which passed directly above our house. Often, as many as six flocks would come over together, heading northwards, and when their last calls had died away on the thin air I would gradually doze off in the long and even silence. 'Cur-leek-leek, curr-leek-leek-leek, cu-r-r-r-r-leek' – they were coming south this time and, drowsy as I was, that shrill, bubbling whistle would send me rushing to the window to peer among the stars and catch the vague shapes as they swept over the hill and down towards the marshes. Then I would fall asleep, wondering whether these were the same birds that passed and re-passed along that aerial road in the night, or whether, by mutual agreement, they were carrying on a system of exchange in the marshes and up and down the coast.

When I went to live inland, I found that what I missed most of all was the calling of sea and marsh birds in the night. There is something sad and strange and lonely in the sudden piercing voice that comes out of the darkness high above you, the voice of a bird travelling at sixty miles an hour, which, when next you hear it, is no more than a distant pipe drifting away over the sleeping village.

Julian Tennyson, *Suffolk Scene*

ANOTHER FOUR MILES of chalk road rising and falling over the open down; more far-reaching vistas of this strange land to the east, and to the west, and to the south; nothing else to be seen but the long billows of green patched here and there upon their sides, or in their troughs, with golden harvest fields, and tufted with the clumps of fir or beech, which in the far distance show merely black specks upon the waste. There are no roadside fences here to break the view, and the low grassy banks which fringe the highway are rank by now with the tall stiff stems and matted undergrowth of cocksfoot, rye-grass, or fescues, and decked in patches here and there with the modest hues of scabious and wild parsley, but mostly powdered white in this August weather by the dust of travelling sheep or the occasional motor. No grouse crow, nor do curlews call, amid these chalk solitudes; nor yet is there anywhere the faintest note of tumbling water. Indeed, the characteristic quality of the Wiltshire downland is, as often as not, its over-powering silence, unless the faint murmur of wild bees may be accounted as a disturbing factor. The sound of a big pine forest stirred by the breeze is always inspiring. But to pass from the utter silence that often reigns among the grave mounds on the high down into the hoarse music of some group of veteran Scotch firs that have braved both years and storms is better still. Yet there is music enough, too, on the downs at times. The young peewits in August have found both voice and winds, and sweep about with lusty cries. The skylark is always here, and often in tuneful mood. But the gregarious sheep of the down is much quieter than the sheep of the Welsh and Northern moorland, who seems always to be proclaiming that he has lost either himself, or a lamb, or his companions.

A. G. Bradley, *Round About Wiltshire*

BUTTERFLIES WERE NUMEROUS and varied; those best remembered being the brimstone, the meadow brown, the blues, the tortoiseshells, the peacocks and the red admirals. The brimstones were always the first butterflies to be seen in spring; the meadow browns were the commonest of all in the fields; the blues were the daintiest and seen throughout the summer in the lanes; the tortoiseshells always came indoors in the autumn and hung themselves up in some corner where they would remain throughout the winter, unless swept away by the turkey-feather brooms which were bought off the gypsies and used to sweep away cobwebs from high corners; the peacocks were not common and their lovely eyed wings always attracted attention; the red admirals were the latest and most lovely of all – they had a great liking for ripe pears and could always be seen in the top garden when the pears began to fall. Another favourite of the lanes was the orange tip. I remember seeing one year a great flock of clouded yellows on a clover field. Whites, of which I do not remember distinguishing the greater from the lesser, were so usual as to excite no interest.

H. S. Joyce, *I Was Born in the Country*

BY THE TIME the sedge-warblers are back in the reed-beds, and the dykes are full of amorous frogs, there is much to tempt one to take a cruise on the rivers or a ramble along the river walls. Every marsh and swampy road is then bright with golden clusters of marsh marigolds; on the sun-warmed sides of the walls yellow coltsfoot has pushed its way up through the clods, and purple patches of dead nettle attract the early roving bees. On the boggy lands green rushes are gradually hiding the withered growths of rush and sedge; the silken sallow catkins are sending out their yellow anthers, and the ruddy bog myrtle fills the air with its sweet, strong scent. Sunward the river is agleam with flashing ripples; elsewhere the water is as blue as the sky. As you cross the rush marshes, redshanks and peewits rise from their nesting-grounds, crying plaintively; now and again a snipe is flushed, and, uttering that strange bleating note which has gained it the name of 'summer lamb', betakes itself to erratic flight. In almost every dyke where there is dead sedge or gladden, moorhens are beginning to make their nests, and the loud challenge of the pugnacious cocks is heard along the riversides; while from the shores of the larger Broads comes the harsh 'cark' of the coot. The reed-beds are full of sedge-warblers, playing the mocking-bird to sparrow, thrush and finch; occasionally a louder, quicker 'chucking' tells of the presence of a reed-warbler. By the time the reed-warblers – which arrive later than the sedge-warblers – are heard, you may listen for the strange insect-like 'reeling' of the shy little grasshopper warblers, which lurk among the scrub of sweet gale and sallow and in the lush marsh grass. On the floating rafts of broken reeds and sedges, with which the wind and tide have covered the surface of some of the creeks, those dignified and graceful little dyke-rangers, the yellow wagtails, are strutting, carefully searching for crawling insects or darting their beaks at those upon the wing. In the marsh farm gardens tits and finches are busy among the fruit-buds, and the goldfinch, which is not so rare in Norfolk as in some counties where the bird-catchers are more in evidence, is often heard singing among the apple trees.

William A. Dutt, *The Norfolk Broads*

30 MAY. WALKING to Marnhull. The prime of bird-singing. The thrushes and blackbirds are the most prominent – pleading earnestly rather than singing, and with such modulation that you seem to see their little tongues curl inside their bills in their emphasis. A bullfinch sings from a tree with a metallic sweetness piercing as a fife.

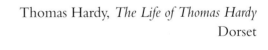

Thomas Hardy, *The Life of Thomas Hardy*
Dorset

ALMOST THE FIRST insect to excite my curiosity was the house cricket, great numbers of which inhabited the cracks in the walls of the bakehouse around the great oven. The crickets were drawn to the bakehouse by the warmth there. They probably also fed on the flour, but this could not have been the main attraction, or they would have been equally plentiful in the mill. When the bakehouse had been unoccupied for an hour or two, the crickets would come to the edge of the crevices between the bricks and sit there 'chirping' so loudly that they could be heard quite clearly as one passed the door. There must have been hundreds of all sizes in the place. They seemed quite tame and, unless one made a sudden movement, would sit at the entrances of their homes and allow themselves to be watched closely. . .

In the garden there were several insects that drew attention to themselves by reason of their size, colouring or habits. Ladybirds were great favourites. We often caught these and, handling them with great care, placed them on our hands and allowed them to climb up our raised fingers. As they did this, we would recite the following lines:

> Ladybird, ladybird, fly away home,
> Your house is on fire, your children are gone.
> All but one that lies under a stone.
> Fly away ladybird, fly away home.

And almost invariably the ladybird raised its red wing-cases, stretched out its gauzy underwings and departed just as the last line was reached.

A snail was usually placed on the ground and threatened as follows:

> Snail, snail, come out of your hole;
> Or I will beat you as black as a coal.

Whereupon the snail would slowly thrust out its horns and head and proceed to crawl away.

H. S. Joyce, *I Was Born in the Country*

ALONG THE STREAM – bordered just there by willows – is a broad band of turf flanked by nut bushes that shelter each a rustic seat, and sparkling in spring with clumps of daffodils, 'Tossing their heads in sprightly dance'.

I often wonder why these flowers thrill not poet and painter alone, but plain individuals like myself, with such a keen and intimate delight. Is the magic to be found in their colour – the very essence of sunshine – or in their suggestion of spring fragrance, for scent they hardly can be said to possess? In truth their charm is too subtle to bear analysing and consists, I think, as much in the impressions they convey to the inward eye as in aught tangible. To me they bring visions of a thousand things: of bright though broken sunlight; of a windy sky across whose April blue race fleecy clouds like white horses across the sea; of skipping lambs and young green corn; of bowing tree-tops whose buds are beginning to show purple; of the first feathery shoots of the larches and the earliest primrose – things of life and hope all. The daffodils in the Red-house garden can be seen by every one passing on the bridge; and when the sun is shining through their golden petals and burnishing the surface of the water, when it is brightening the pink willow-buds and revealing unsuspected tints in the mossy trunks of the apple trees beyond the brook, that little strip of grass is a joy, the remembrance of which abides throughout the year, until the changing months make it once again something more than a memory.

Eleanor G. Hayden, *Travels Round Our Village*
Berkshire

I NEVER TIRED of listening to even the poorest of the characteristic species; even the common bunting was a constant pleasure. In the wide sunny world I preferred him to his neighbour and relation, the yellow-hammer. The sound he emits by way of song is certainly bright, and, like some other bird-voices, it is associated in my mind with hot and brilliant weather with the appearance of water spouting or leaping and sparkling in the sun. Doubtless such expressions as 'needles of sound', 'splinters', and 'shafts', and 'jets of sound', etc., to be found in writers on bird music, are not wholly metaphorical, but actually express the connection existing in the writer's mind between certain sounds and sights. The common bunting's little outburst of confused or splintered notes is when heard (by me) at the same time mentally seen as a handful of clear water thrown up and breaking into sparkling drops in the sunlight.

W. H. Hudson, *Nature in Downland*
Sussex

THE VILLAGE

June 21st. Went to stay for three days at Plympton four miles from Plymouth; the vegetation there is much more luxuriant than on the heights of Dartmoor.

Edith Holden, *The Nature Notes of an Edwardian Lady*

Visitors to the countryside wrote about landscape; but it is usually in the accounts of the villagers themselves that we find the true flavour of day-to-day village life in Victorian and Edwardian Britain. The pattern of the daily social round was linked to the life of the seasons; it was a world that was largely to disappear as the century progressed, and increased mobility meant the dissemination of a populace that had, by and large, remained relatively static for centuries. Before the coming of the car and the train, a man or woman could live their whole life within the compass of a few miles. A shepherd moving to another village over the down in search of work might find himself in a strange new world, where the voices, customs, habits – even the soil – were alien, bewildering and forbidding.

Inevitably it was in the villages' commercial places that social life was lived most visibly, and that, as often as not, meant the village shop. For Lilian Bond, remembering the lost Dorset village of Tyneham, it was the blend of smells that triggered the memory ever after, but there were many other powerful reminders as the old order faded. The contrast of boisterous vibrant life and almost awesome rural stillness is one which provides us today with a strong image of rural community life in a bygone age. Today there is almost always the rumble of traffic on a distant road, or the glow in the night-time sky from a far-off town. To sit with H. S. Joyce at a village concert, or to walk out with Edward Thomas into the darkening village street, is to be part of a belovedly insular existence in which many a village was a microcosm of the larger world beyond.

THERE IS THE village in my mind's eye, as it was . . . the age-long routine of Cornish life still unbroken, though perhaps like an old grandfather clock it was winding down slowly, imperceptibly, to a stop. The War – till lately 'the War' still meant in these parts the Great War of 1914–18: evidence perhaps of the slowness of adaptation, the tenacity of our minds – the War brought all that life of habit to a sudden full stop, held it suspended, breathless for a full four years in the shadow of its wing, and meanwhile set in being motions and tendencies which came to full flood the moment the War was over and swept away the old landmarks in a tide of change . . . In the pre-war years of which I am writing, the continuity of custom was still unbroken. One thing of interest to the social historian, for example: the families, the family names which for generations and even for centuries had belonged to some particular spot had not yet been disturbed, uprooted by the revolution in transport. Though many Cornish families sent a large quota of their sons abroad, to the United States and South Africa especially, the parent stock remained at home in the old place. So there were always Jenkinses at Phernyssick, Pascoes at Holmbush, Tretheweys at Roche; Kellows, Blameys, Rowses at Tregonissey. Now as I write, there is neither a Kellow nor a Blamey nor a Rowse at Tregonissey any more. The old social structure has at length been broken, like a pitcher at the well, the pieces dispersed. And the same with many of the old customs and ways.

A. L. Rowse, *A Cornish Childhood*

LIFE [IN THE VILLAGE] IS full of a beautiful broad simplicity and directness. It deals more with essentials than refinements. One finds the genuinely human there, with less disguise than in the cities, where men conceal their individualities under a mask of uniformity. In the village, people are frankly natural. This simplicity is far removed from the ignoble, for its sincerity gives it dignity. The world is so small there that everyone has his distinct place in it, and the result is not a narrowing one on the individual. Rather he is impressed with a serious sense of his responsibilities, of the awful importance of the part he plays. It is when our world is so wide that it dwarfs us to pigmies, that we are apt to become irresponsible and frivolous.

Stewart Dick, *The Cottage Homes of England*

IT IS GOOD in these days of bustle and strife to drift for a while into some quiet backwater – such as may yet be found in rural England – which the tide of progress stirs but just enough to avert stagnation; where old-world customs and archaic forms of speech still linger and where men go about their daily tasks in a spirit of serene leisureliness, therein copying Nature who never hurries. Of such a sequestered corner, its humours, its homely comedies and simple pathos would I write.

Eleanor G. Hayden, *Travels Round Our Village*
Berkshire

THE HOME OF my childhood, eternal and green, appears before my inward eye, and I live again in the brightly coloured circle of hills where I was born. No matter where I am, I seek unconsciously for resemblances to that beloved spot. A draught of spring water, an uncut hedgerow, a broken wall, these bring back visions so real that I cannot tell in which life I am living, the present, or the crystal-clear past, when as a child I ran with arms outstretched to catch the wind down the well-known grassy hillsides.

Alison Uttley, *Country World*
Derbyshire

THE ALLOTMENTS BECAME a most important part of the cottager's life. A stock of potatoes could now be grown and stored against each winter; it became possible to grow and fat a pig and to hang its flitches on the cottage walls. To these ends every available hour – except Sunday – throughout the spring, summer and autumn was given to their cultivation; and often, when the work was in arrears, the husband would rise early and put in an hour or two before beginning labour on the farm at seven.

The allotment fields of the village resembled the preceding open-field system; the rood strips, side by side, were, in miniature, like the former acre strips. Throughout the long summer evenings, someone would be seen working on each, often husband and wife with the older children of the family. Many roods were planted with corn – wheat for the family loaves and puddings, or barley for the pig in the sty; but the potato crop was important beyond any other. Many labourers rented two or more roods, and thus were able to grow both corn and vegetables. In that way the standard of life was improved; but it is clear at the same time that it made it possible to accept the less-than-living-wage for longer than it would otherwise have lasted.

The plots were cultivated well, and the rents were properly paid. It was, in fact, an order of life that proved natural to them all. The sacrifice and toil involved brought a new outlook on life; to become the tenant of the rood of land, though by payment of rent, was an act of independence that found a ready response in native character; it preserved a meaning to life above that of merely working for a wage.

Walter Rose, *Good Neighbours*
Buckinghamshire

I USED TO live with my parents in a very busy little sweet shop. At first we only sold sweets, but during the summer my mother used to make her own ice-cream. Every week, or probably twice a week in the hot weather, we used to have an enormous block of ice brought to the shop. They used to go to the butcher across the road and leave some there. She had to chop this up into little pieces and put it into a machine and grind it up. It was most beautiful ice-cream. It came out of the tub in the middle and the ice was round it.

There were lots of people coming in at night, into the back place, sitting there eating all kinds of ice-creams with various syrups over them which she used to make herself. The ice-cream was made with Bird's custard powder and fresh cream which was bought from Mr Green's farm at Wenny. He used to bring it fresh, sometimes twice a day. What the other ingredients were I don't know – she used to keep it secret.

When I was put to bed it was very lonely because they were so busy in the shop. In the bedroom there was a little hole in the floor which was an airway to the window below. I used to be out of bed every few minutes and shout, 'Daddy, are you there?' He used to shout up, 'Go to sleep, I'm here!'

You could get lovely Golden Charm toffees for 2*d*. a quarter ... If a gentleman had his sweetheart with him, my father would say, 'Would you like a Dorothy bag?' – and for 3*d*. extra you could have it in a little velvet bag, so it made a present for his sweetheart.

Vera Connolly, *We're the Characters Now*
Cambridgeshire

LYDIA FRENCH HAD a shop opposite the church. The little town or overgrown village had no market, but there were fairs held in the space before the church on one side and Lydia French's shop on the other twice in the year. Both were cattle fairs, frequented by farmers. On such occasions bullocks ran about with tails lifted, yelling men and barking dogs behind and before them, and made either for the churchyard wall or for Lydia French's shop window. The Oddfellows, moreover, held their annual feast there, and processionized behind a band, and waved banners and wore sashes, and ate and drank heartily at the Peal of Bells. On such occasions stalls were erected in the open space, where nuts were shot for, and barley-sugar-sticks and twisted peppermint rods and brandy-balls were sold, also gingerpop and lemonade. On all these occasions Lydia French's shop was full of customers. She, moreover, had

a good clientele in the entire parish, but experienced less difficulty in disposing of her goods than in getting her little bills paid.

Sabine Baring Gould, *In a Quiet Village*
Devon

THERE WAS NO place quite so welcome on a cold day as the bakehouse; it was always warm and cosy in there. Local people often stopped during a shower to take refuge in the stables, which opened right on to the main road; but, if it was really cold weather, many of those who could claim any sort of acquaintance with Father, turned off the road and went into the bakehouse to enjoy the warmth and have a chat before continuing their journey.

The bakehouse was a low, square building with a window looking straight out on to the river . . . The oven stood nearly opposite the door. A stout iron door closed its mouth and inside was a deep and low cavern paved with flat stones. It was heated chiefly with faggots of furze cut on the downs and kept in stacks on the spare ground between the mill and the river . . . When the faggots had burnt themselves out, the door of the oven was opened and any embers that remained were raked out

by means of a long-handled iron tool, curved at the end into a half circle. These embers were thrown into a recess at floor level below and slightly to one side of the oven. Sufficient heat remained in them to stew things slowly, and frequently an iron pot filled with small potatoes stood over them. The cooked potatoes were used as food for the pigs and poultry. A second implement was used to clear out the small embers still remaining in the oven and to cool the floor slightly. This consisted of a long pole to which was attached a short length of chain and a piece of sacking. The sacking was dipped in water and then pushed and turned about over the floor of the oven until every glowing cinder had been 'douted' and swept out. The oven was now ready to receive the batch of loaves.

H. S. Joyce, *I Was Born in the Country*

THE COTTAGE WOMEN when they went shopping were the despair of the drapers. A woman, with two or three more to chorus her sentiments, would go into a shop and examine half-a-dozen dress fabrics, rubbing each between her work-hardened fingers and thumb till the shopkeeper winced, expecting to see it torn. After trying several and getting the counter covered she would push them aside, contemptuously remarking, 'I don't like this yer shallygallee (flimsy) stuff. Haven't 'ee got any gingham tackle?' Whereat the poor draper would cast down a fresh roll of stoutest material with the reply: 'Here, madam. Here's something that will wear like pinwire.' This did better, but was declared to be 'gallus dear'.

Richard Jefferies, *Hamlet Folk*
Wiltshire

IN MY YOUNG days the parish shop was the one market for the village, augmented by a kipper and bloater gentleman with a pony – or donkey – cart, and by a butcher and coal merchant from a rather larger village adjacent. My own mother had a large storeroom, which contained a variety of gigantic jars (rather like the jars which hid the robbers in the fairytale of *Ali Baba*), in which reposed currants, sultanas, sugar and other delicacies. A small hand could just reach down – and clutch firmly!

B. Knyvet Wilson, *More Norfolk Tales*

ROGER GILES – SURGUN, Parish Clark and Schulemaster, Grocer and Hundertaker, respectfully informs ladies and gentlemans that he drors teef without waiting a minute, applies laches every hour, blisters on the lowest terms, and vissicks for a penny a piece. He sells Godfathers Krodales, kuts corns, bunyons, doctors hosses, and clips donkeys wance a munth, and undertakes to look after everybody's navls by the ear. Joesharps, penny wissels, brass kannelsticks, frying pans and other moosical hinstruments hat greatly reduced figers. Young ladies and gentlemen larnes their grammar and langeudge in the purtiest manner, also grate care taken of their morrels and spelling. Also zarm singing, tayching base vile and other fancy sorts of work, squadrils, pokers, weazels and all country dances toit at home and abroad at perfeksun. Perfumery and snuff in all its branches. As times is cruel bad I beg to tell ee that I has just beginned to sell all sorts of stationery ware, cox, hens, fouls, pigs and all other kinds of poultry, blackin brishes, herrins, coles, scrubbin brishes, traykel and godley bukes and bibles, mise traps, brickdist, whisker seeds, morrell pokkerankerchers and all sorts of swatemaits, includin taters, sasages and other garden stuff, bakky zizars, lamp oyle, tay kittles and other intoxzikatin likkers, a dale of fruit, hats, zongs hair oyle, pattins, bukkets, grandin stones and other aitables, korne and bunyon salve and all hardware. I has laid in a large assortment of tripe, dogs mate, lollipops, ginger beer, matches and other pikkles such as hepsom salts, hoysters, Winser sope, anzetrar – Old rages bort and sold here and nowhere else, new laid eggs by me Roger Giles; Zinging burdes keeped, such as howles, donkeys, paycox, lobsters, crickets, also a stock of celebrated brayder.

P.S. – I tayches geography, ritmitmetic, cowsticks, jimnastics and other Cheynees tricks.

Bonny Sartin, A Little Bit of Dorset

THE SHOP HAD a fine, rich blend of smells, bacon and cheese predominating, with alluring undercurrents of tea, liquorice and peppermint. There was a varied choice of biscuits to be had at popular prices. (I specially remember 'butter creams', juicy and toothsome at three halfpence a quarter), and chocolate and sweets to suit all comers. Fry's chocolate cream was on sale in big, thick bars at a penny apiece and penn'orth of sugared almonds, bulls' eyes, acid drops, fruit jellies and the like filled a sizeable bag. There were comfits, too, in different shapes and colours, bearing

romantic legends: 'Will you be my sweetheart?', 'I love you', 'Will you be mine?' . . . and jars full of mammoth peppermint humbugs. Ha'porths were served just as willingly as were the larger amounts, and a fat bag of popcorn was sold for a farthing. In fact, a penny spelt riches when spent at the shop.

Lilian Bond, *Tyneham: A Lost Heritage*
Dorset

I WENT OUT into the village at about half-past nine in the dark, quiet evening. A few stars penetrated the soft sky; a few lights shone on earth, from a distant farm seen through a gap in the cottages. Single and in groups, separated by gardens or bits of orchard, the cottages were vaguely discernible; here and there a yellow window square gave out a feeling of home, tranquillity, security. Nearly all were silent. Ordinary speech was not to be heard, but from one house came the sounds of an harmonium being played and a voice singing a hymn, both faintly. A dog barked far off. After an interval a gate fell to lightly. Nobody was on the road.

The road was visible most dimly, and was like a pale mist at an uncertain distance. When I reached the green all was still and silent. The cottages on the opposite side of the road all lay back, and they were merely blacker stains on the darkness. The

pollard willows fringing the green, which in the sunlight resemble mops, were now very much like a procession of men, strange primaeval beings, pausing to meditate in the darkness.

The intervals between the cottages were longer here, and still longer; I ceased to notice them until I came to the last house, a small farm, where the dog growled, but in a subdued tone, as if only to condemn my footsteps on the deserted road.

Rows of elm trees on both sides of the road succeeded. I walked more slowly, and at a gateway stopped. While I leaned looking over it at nothing, there was a long silence that could be felt, so that a train whistling two miles away seemed as remote as the stars. The noise could not overleap the boundaries of that silence. And yet I presently moved away, back towards the village, with slow steps.

I was tasting the quiet and safety without a thought. Night had no evil in it. Though a stranger, I believed that no one wished to harm me. The first man I saw, fitfully revealed by a swinging lantern as he crossed his garden, seemed to me to have the same feeling, to be utterly free of trouble or any care. A man slightly drunk deviated towards me, halted muttering, and deviated away again. I heard his gate shut, and he was absorbed.

The inn door, which was now open, was as the entrance to a bright cave in the middle of the darkness: the illumination had a kind of blessedness such as it might have had to a cow, not without foreignness; and a half-seen man within it belonged to a world, blessed indeed, but far different from this one of mine, dark, soft and tranquil. I felt that I could walk on thus, sipping the evening silence and solitude, endlessly. But at the house where I was staying, I stopped as usual. I entered, blinked at the light, and by laughing at something, said with the intention of being laughed at, I swiftly again naturalized myself.

Edward Thomas, *In Pursuit of Spring*
Somerset

A LONG, LOW building bordering on the green, with some patient old folk sitting in the vine-clad porches or tending their flowers, is the almshouse of the village, erected by an ancestor of the present squire in Tudor times. He had gathered much wealth out of the spoils of the monasteries, and thought he ought to spend some of his increased riches on the infirm old folk of his village. He built also a grammar school for the young people, but it has seen better days, and is only an elementary school now.

P. H. Ditchfield, *Rural England*

THE NARROW FOOTWAY took us on to Cleeve Priors and through its street – a village all sober, grey and beautiful. The garden walls, coated with lichen and topped with yellow quinces or a flaming branch of barberry; the tall church tower; the quaintly elaborate gravestones below it, their scrolls and cherubim overgrown with moss; the clipped yew trees that abounded in all fantastic shapes; the pigeons wheeling round their dovecote, and the tall poplar by the manor farm – all these were good: but best of all was the manor farm itself, and the arched yew hedge leading to its Jacobean porch, a marvel to behold. We hung long about the entrance and stared at it. But no living man or woman approached us. The village was given up to peace or sleep or death.

Sir Arthur Quiller-Couch, *The Warwickshire Avon*

THE VILLAGE CONCERTS were really great fun; friends met and chatted together as they came in, for everyone from the surrounding district attended. The schoolroom was the usual place at which all village meetings were held; often it was the only place available. Before the performance started there was a continual rustling of skirts and scraping of chairs as the earlier arrivals turned to check in those coming later. At the back, admitted for a penny or twopence, were the farm labourers, gardeners, coachmen and local artisans, usually accompanied by their wives and often their children. Probably the vicar opened the proceedings with a short speech of welcome and a description of the objects of the entertainment and details of the fund that was to benefit. If possible the first item would be a pianoforte duet; if a duet pair could not be found, there would be a pianoforte solo. Then followed a varied assortment of songs, recitations and instrumental music; great care being taken to see that the item that followed a comic number was not one that would be too much overshadowed by the general appeal of the comic. Sometimes monologues, duologues, or even One-Act Plays helped out the performance. Plays were without exception either comedies or farces, the latter for preference. I never once saw a serious attempt at straight acting in any of these concerts.

H. S. Joyce, *I Was Born in the Country*

DURING SUMMER THE village, with the exception of a few houses near the upper end, is almost invisible to the passing wayfarer on the high road, since at this season of the year it retires into the leafy concealment of its gardens and orchards. The roofs of thatch, tiles or slates are hidden by a mass of verdure that viewed from afar, before the sickle has touched the ripened grain, looks like an emerald set in gold. Around on every side spreads a well-nigh unbroken sea of yellow corn, and here and there from the quivering undulating waves rise scattered patches of woodland, dark and motionless as islands. The distance is veiled by a delicate blue haze; over the whole expanse a slumberous stillness broods. The traveller might almost fancy he had reached the lotus-eaters' land, where it is always afternoon.

Eleanor G. Hayden, *Travels Round Our Village*
Berkshire

WHIT MONDAY WAS a wonderful day. We had a band in church, a large brass band, and then we went out of the church and had a big tea, and then after the tea we marched along with the band all the way to a field where we had races for children. We enjoyed Whit Monday like anything. It was a wonderful day.

Mercy Summerhayes, *The Nineties*
Gloucestershire

ON THE FARM

June 16. Saw the first field of grass down, and cutting-machines at work in several clover-fields.

Edith Holden, *The Country Diary of an Edwardian Lady*

The farm was – and is – the institution around which rural life has always resolved. There have of course been changes, many of which happened between the years 1890 and 1914. Threshing machines became common, and they brought with them a new way of working. Nevertheless it was a work-style that continued to involve the whole farm community, although there is little doubt that the older generation looked askance at these noisy smoking monsters. After all, for a man aged seventy in late Victorian Britain, there would be family memories of the machine-breaking riots of the 1830s.

The rural folk-memory went back even further: to the naming of fields, and an intimate knowledge of the local terrain fed by a continuing presence in one place of generation upon generation from a single family. In the first years of the twentieth century, increased mobility began to change things. Country-dwellers began to

gravitate to the towns, while town-dwellers gained more access to the country. The annual hop-picking in Kent became one of the few opportunities to escape into the fresh air for many Londoners as they poured out into the country for a working holiday, helped on their way by an ever-improving transport system.

Animals were seldom far away on the farm, and as with other elements of rural life, the partnership between man and beast was a practical one that left little room for sentimentality. This is not to say that there was no sense of kinship: on the contrary. A. C. Benson was to note how 'cows bring tranquillity into the spirit', while Hannah Hauxwell saw the animals as her playmates, recalling them with affection, just as A. B. Tinsley was to remember the lamp-lit serenity of the barton, and the gentle puffing of the contented cattle, safe for the night, with their 'turnip-sweet breath' misting the frosty air.

COWS BRING DEEP tranquillity into the spirit; their glossy skins, their fragrant breath, their contented ease, their mild gaze, their Epicurean rumination tend to restore the balance of the mind . . . There is the dignity of innocence about the cow, and I often wish that she did not bear so poor a name, a word so unsuitable for poetry; it is lamentable that one has to take refuge in the archaism of 'kine' when the thing itself is so gentle and pleasant.

A. C. Benson, *The Thread of Gold*

THERE WAS LITTLE farm machinery used in those days. 'Hand work is best work,' my master used to say, and he did not like to have even a horse in the field. Corn was cut with a short 'badging' hook and hay was cut with the scythe. A man could cut half an acre of corn a day and bind it into sheaves, but usually the farmers banded themselves together and worked in groups of from twelve to twenty . . . How country folk laughed when the first machines appeared.

Tom Mullins: John Burnett, *Useful Toil*
Staffordshire

THE FIELD NAMES gave the clue to the fields' history. Near the farmhouse, 'Moat Piece', 'Fishponds', 'Duffus [i.e. dovehouse] Piece', 'Kennels' and 'Warren Piece' spoke of a time before the Tudor house took the place of another and older establishment. Farther on, 'Lark Hill', 'Cuckoos Clump', 'The Osiers' and 'Pond Piece' were named after natural features, while 'Gibbard's Piece' and 'Blackwell's' probably commemorated otherwise long-forgotten former occupants. The large new fields round the hamlet had been cut too late to be named and were known as 'The Hundred Acres', 'The Sixty Acres', and so on according to their acreage. One or two of the ancients persisted in calling one of these 'The Heath' and another 'The Racecourse'.

One name was as good as another to most of the men; to them it was just a name and meant nothing. What mattered to them about the fields in which they happened to be working was whether the road was good or bad which led them from the farm to it; or if it was comparatively sheltered or one of those bleak open places which the wind hurtled through, driving the rain through the clothes to the very pores; and was the soil easily workable or of back-breaking heaviness or so bound together with that 'hemmed' twitch that a ploughshare could scarcely get through it.

There were usually three or four ploughs to a field, each of them drawn by a team of three horses, with a boy at the head of the leader and the ploughman behind at the shafts. All day, up and down they would go, ribbing the pale stubble with stripes of dark furrows, which, as the day advanced, would get wider and nearer together, until, at length, the whole field lay a rich velvety plum-colour.

Flora Thompson, *Lark Rise to Candleford*
Oxfordshire

BEFORE BEING ALLOWED to enter stables and cowsheds, I was always warned to keep well clear of the animals' hind feet, because, being small, I could easily be mistaken for a dog trotting along behind them. But, in spite of this warning, I was once laid low by a well-placed kick between the eyes from a mature milking cow, one summer evening. This unkind act resulted in my being rushed indoors to have attention in the shape of rural first aid, which culminated in my going to bed with a vinegar-and-brown-paper dressing on the bruise.

Cow-kine, as most farming folk know, are curious creatures; they can become as friendly and affectionate as a 'cade' lamb, if given encouragement, yet they never get on such terms with each other. Though they keep together in small or large herds, there is always an order of seniority which is rigidly adhered to, as can be seen when a herd passes through a gateway.

Perhaps this order of leadership springs from a female tendency to exaggerate the importance of minor matters. The old bull amongst the herd didn't give two hoots whether he came first or last through the gate.

During winter months, all the cattle were kept indoors at night and food was fed to them in their 'booseys' or cribs, in the form of pulped turnip, hay or crushed corn. The safe 'folding' of all the cattle on a stormy winter night always sent a thrill through me. It seemed like the pulling of a castle drawbridge, signifying that all within the walls were safe and cared for.

Just before bedtime, a visit would be paid to all the animals in their various buildings, to ensure that they were safe and in no danger from their tethers, that is, that they were not hanging in their tie-chains.

On frosty nights the warm, turnip-sweet breath of each animal would rise, like steam from a kettle. The chinking of tie-chains, puffs and snorts, all contributed to the picture illuminated by the ubiquitous hurricane lamp at this important time of 'supping up', as it was known.

A. B. Tinsley, *Horse and Cart Days*
Shropshire

As I was the only child, the animals were my playmates. We had sheep, cows, horses, dogs and pigs. The pigs were my favourites. Most people think pigs are dirty and ignorant, but I had many happy times with them. I was even allowed to look after two piglets on my own; they were very intelligent and affectionate.

Hannah Hauxwell, *Country Living*
Yorkshire Dales

Though Stratford Mop, said to be the largest statute fair in England, has almost lost its original character, it retains some of its old features, and is still regarded by the agricultural class in the district as the chief holiday of the year.

It is one of the few remaining fairs at which a custom nearly as old as the hills is still carried out – the custom mentioned in the Cumberland ballad:

> *At Carel [Carlisle] I stuid wi' a strae i' my mooth;*
> *The weyves com' roun' me in custers.*
> *'What weage dus te ax, canny lad?' ses yen.*

So men commonly stood for hire in the days of ancient Rome, and down through the centuries till quite recently. Even in London, in the latter part of the eighteenth century, there were recognized markets – Cheapside and Charing Cross – for men in the building trade, who carried their respective tools as a badge or mark of their particular occupation.

The custom was general at hiring fairs. Except, however, at Stratford, Banbury – where grooms carry a bit of straw in their buttonhole, shepherds a twist of wool, carters a length of whipcord – and a few other places, it is now extinct. At Stratford the demand for whipcord, the trade mark of the carter, is such that men hawk it in the street. But even in Shakespeare's town the maids, who formerly stood for hire like the men, now resort to the registry office.

Several derivations are given of the word 'mop'. The mop seems to have been at one time a second hiring fair, at which the refuse from the first was mopped or swept up.

Michael MacDonagh, *Records of National Life and History*
Warwickshire

THE HOP GARDEN was on the southern border of the farm, beyond the great oaks of Blooming Meadow in which the house stood, and it was a pleasant walk, just as far as the children, who were babies, could manage. Over the meadow by the hedge, through the gap by the pond, and there you were.

I had watched from the early time of the year the cultivation of the hops, involving a variety of skills, from the ploughing with horses between the 'hills' – the perennial hop plants of which nothing could be seen in winter but the slightly rounded mounds stretching away in symmetrical rows – to the delicate 'twiddling' of the bines when the shoots appeared and had to be trained to the strings which had already been stretched criss-cross from pole to pole. The strings made an intricate design, seeming to envelop the garden in a glowing mist . . .

The picking on our farm was done by village women and children . . . For us the only men to give zest to the bawdy jokes which the atmosphere of this harvest evoked, even in the most chapel-minded women, were the tally-men, perhaps six to this small garden. These men had much to do. It was their job to cut, with the razor-edged sickle-shaped knife at the end of a long pole, the bines from the strings and drape these armfuls of hop-laden tendrils over the bar of wood raised above the trough so that the pickers could loosen the tangle and rob its fruit, dropping each hop separately – never in bunches – into the bin . . .

At noon the horn would sound and we must finish picking the bine we had in hand, for to begin a new one was forbidden. Now the tally-man came with his bushel-basket to measure the hops each picker had in her trough, and with a lovely gesture the women plunged their bare arms deep into their cargo and with a sort of flutter of the hands and fingers raised the heavy load to let the air and space into their packing, so that the precious fruit would go lightly into the tally-man's measure and pile up to the bushel mark more quickly. With what keen eyes they watched his measure, for pay was by the bushel. I think the pay for my pick entered in the tally-man's book was sixpence.

Now with our appetites whetted by the heady hop-impregnated air we sat around our bins for lunch. This consisted of the traditional bottles of cold tea and slabs of baked bread pudding full of fruit and brown sugar, sticky and extremely satisfying. We sat on the hard clay, enjoying the food and laughing and talking. The children got restive when they had eaten their fill and played hide-and-seek in the still untouched bowers, and the suckled babies were changed and put back in their prams. The women's rough and golden-stained hands were for a moment idle. Looking away down the avenue of green leaves I could glimpse brightly coloured groups of women and children in attitudes of repose and presently a silence would fall under that fruit-laden darkness of leaves and the children would curl up by their mothers and sleep, and the women, unused to idleness, would nod. The tally-men lay flat out on their backs with heads resting on their upraised hands, and there would

be no sound but the murmur of insects and distant lowing of cattle. Such a scene, such a quality of living enriched my spirit for ever.

Helen Thomas, *A Remembered Harvest*
Kent

AMONG THE RED-LETTER days of youth I count threshing day supreme. The huge engine and tall drum, the box van and iron water-tank lurched drunkenly down the lane, missed the overhang of the barn roof by inches and came to rest in the field behind the barn. When winter mud surrounded the barn my cup of joy overflowed because they always got stuck fast. Iron skid-pans were bolted to the wheels and Bill said, 'Let 'er 'ave it'. A wire rope and the engine winch, aided by Bill's pungent vocabulary, yanked the drum through the clinging clay on to the barn floor. The way the yard was churned up during this 'setting up' process was nobody's business – nor were some of the words I learned until I repeated them to my aunt. Anticipating the event, five hundredweight of Welsh steam coal lay ready for the engine.

By seven a.m. the following day the long belt was put on and the droning task-master began sucking down sheaves of corn. As 'cider-boy' I was popular up to a point, but sent off with a 'flea in my ear' when I got too cocky. At nightfall they packed up and drew out ready for a six a.m. departure, and the driver, to my intense indignation, packed all the remaining steam coal into his bunker.

But when all was quiet and Bill had gone to the local to send something chasing my cider, my aunt and I crept out to the rear of the drum. Opening up the little slides we ran out every grain of wheat – our wheat, mind you – that Bill, as he cleaned the machine, had carefully kept back for his hens. A fitting end to an exciting day.

Reg Gammon, *One Man's Furrow*
Hampshire

IN THE SUMMER green meat had to be cut; the carter did this with his scythe, the boy loaded it on a dung cart. This green meat, as they named it, consisted of tares, clover and triflomen – a very pretty red kind of clover. Some of it was cut and mixed with hay chaff and the wheat chaff which was saved when thrashing the corn. All chaff cut, hay and straw to be put in the stable, then home. The carters had their tea and came back to the stable to finish and clean the horses and make them comfortable for the night. They called this racking them up for the night. I suppose they named it racking up because hay was put into the hay rack and a mangel or swede or two in the manger for them.

Gaius Carley, *The Memoirs of Gaius Carley*
Sussex

AFTER THE PLOUGH had done its part, the horse-drawn roller was used to break down the clods; then the harrow to comb out and leave in neat piles the weeds and the twitch grass which infested those fields, to be fired later and fill the air with the light blue haze and the scent that can haunt for a lifetime. Then seed was sown, crops were thinned out and hoed and, in time, mown, and the whole process began again.

Flora Thompson, *Lark Rise to Candleford*
Oxfordshire

IN CUMBERLAND THE ploughman calls 'Hop ower' or 'Hop in' to his horses when he wants them to turn to the right, and 'Gee back', 'Whoa back' or 'Wove back' when they are to turn to the left. In Norfolk it is 'Wheesh' for a turn to the right, and 'Cop y holt' or 'Cup yere' for one to the left. In Dorset the cries are 'Get off' and 'Come here'; and in Gloucester, 'Woot' and Coom-yeh'. Each county has its own version, and the ploughman, if he is working with familiar horses, often utters an inarticulate shout or oath quite unintelligible to the stranger passing on the other side of the hedge.

Anon

A CERTAIN NORFOLK man laid out sixpence in a raffle at the local horticultural show. To his great gratification he won first prize – a goat. He led it home in triumph. The same evening several of his friends paid him a visit of congratulation. 'They tell me yew ha' done well, George,' said one. 'Yew ha' won an owd goot, ha'en't ye?' 'Ah! I hev an all,' said George; 'and thass a good goot, that is.' 'Come on then, George, less we hev a look at 'um.' But George was very mysterious. 'He's all right, I ha' gor'um.' 'Well, where is he?' said John. 'Well, thass like this hare,' said George: 'there ha' bin a lot o' these owd tarkey thieves about o' late and I hev a mind to keep my owd goot, so I ha' put him away safe.' 'Well, then, where ha' ye put 'um?' said John. 'I ha' gor'um in the Missis' and my bedroom,' said George. 'Coo! my heart alive! George,' said John. 'What about the *smell*?' 'Well there, John,' said George, 'th' owd goot doan't fare to mind that a mite!'

B. Knyvet Wilson, *More Norfolk Tales*

ON THE DOWNS we heard the reapers chanting a song in the motionless corn. All day they reaped, reaped, and never turned to behold the sun, in whose rebounding beams their faces whitened, whilst their napes and shoulders became brown as they stooped. Sometimes they seemed to hail the sun with wistful pity for their babies, and even for the feverish blossoms. To the sun, which had been gracious to them all the year, and now was cruel, they were praying that he would still be kind; for then, after he was gone, or at least when they saw him not, in the muffled winter, they would suspend a fruited branch of his own ripening over the chimneypiece, thankfully in memoriam; or if he would not listen, they seemed to say, in half-laughing indignation, they would evoke a rain-shower that should veil his glory before evening, or trample upon his triumphs at dawn. But evermore the burden was – that where the reapers reaped, as with the valleys where he raised up a beatific haze. Now charging angrily at the corn rows with sickles, now resting a minute, the reapers presently disappeared in the gulfs they hewed. The women piled the harvest in shining heaps, and after nightfall travelled home, caryatid-like, with children upon their arms, a faggot upon their heads, and the wreck of sunset was gathered round them with a pomp which in human things we should call grandiose.

Edward Thomas, *Rose Acre Papers*
Kent

MOST EMPLOYERS, WHEN harvest was over, gave a supper for their workers; the man for whom my parents worked for over thirty years gave one jointly with two or three other farmers. A big brick and tiled barn was swept out, the cobwebs were brushed down from the rafters, rows of trestle tables were set up down the middle of the building and a platform was put up at one end. Plenty of beer was brought in and huge joints of roast beef and pork provided the main part of the supper which was served by the labourers' wives, a man at each table carving the joints.

When the meal was over, 'our' farmer and the others who were giving the feast with him each made a little speech thanking everyone for all the work that had been done and when each man had had his say there would be loud shouts of 'For he's a jolly good fellow, and so say all of us' – though probably only the day before some of the workers had been calling him, under their breath, anything but a good fellow. Then some of the older harvestmen used to get up and make a speech, though what they said could hardly be called great oratory. One old man, I remember, could only just manage to stammer out:

'If yew young fellas was to dew a bit more like our good Ma-aster dew, there wouldn't be so many on yer dew as yew dew dew' before he sat down, overcome by his great effort.

The speeches ended, Fiddler Brown and an accordion player named Loggins would then strike up a tune and everyone would march round the tables singing, 'Hayman, Strawman, Raggedy-Arse, Maliserman', and this would start the entertainment part of the evening. Plenty of comic songs were sung, plenty of beer was drunk and there was dancing, too, one man at least sure to do a Broomstick Dance by holding a besom in front of him and moving forwards, at each step putting first one leg and then the other over the broom. This needed some doing, especially if the dancer had a good lot of beer in him, if he was not to trip and fall flat on his face.

Arthur Randell: Enid Porter, *Fenland Memories*

THE WEATHER

January 23. Sharp frost and thick fog in the early morning. The fog cleared off about 9.30 a.m. and the sun shone brightly. Went for a country walk. Every twig on every tree and bush was outlined in silver tracery against the sky; some of the dead grasses and seed-vessels growing by the roadside were specially beautiful, every detail of them sparkling with frosty crystals in the sunshine.

Edith Holden, *The Country Diary of an Edwardian Lady*

The weather has always been one of our favourite topics, and not without reason. To the countryman and -woman, the balance of the seasons was the fact upon which all livelihood was based. To the urban visitor, the emphasis was different; it was a nuisance if it was bad, it helped create an idyll if it was good. In this sense the weather became an adjunct of the landscape itself: one made the other, but one also became a *part* of the other – such as mist over the fells, or the 'blue and white and golden days' that unexpectedly light a wintery Oxfordshire meadow-scene.

It is hardly surprising that rain features so much in the passages, but it is interesting to see how it could stimulate writers to such heights of description. The countryman could read the signs; he knew through knowledge and through lore what was coming, when it was time to cover a rick, when the cattle must be attended to and so on. But in the end, there was nothing to do but find shelter, watch and hope. The elements made our rural ancestors what they were: the biting winds, the cutting frosts and the baking sun – all these things carved and lined and shaped the faces that look out from the photographs of pre-First World War rural Britain. The professional writers of Edwardian England who saw only the sunshine of the golden days before the First World War often went home with an image of some sort of illuminated Eden. But the sun did not always shine – by no means . . .

THE FINEST DAYS, when the trees are greenest, the sky bluest and the clouds most snowy white are the days that come in the midst of bad weather. And just as there is no rest without toil, no peace without war, no true joy in life without grief, no enjoyment for the *blasé*, so there can be no lovely summer days without previous storms and rain, no sunshine till the tearful mists have passed away.

There had been a week's incessant rain; every wild flower and every blade of green grass was soaked with moisture, until it could no longer bear its load, and drooped to earth in sheer dismay. But last night there came a change: the sun went down beyond the purple hills like a ball of fire; eastwards the woods were painted with a reddish glow, and life and colour returned to everything that grows on the face of this beautiful earth.

J. Arthur Gibbs, *A Cotswold Village*
Gloucestershire

TODAY HAS BEEN one of those rare blue and white and golden days which sometimes come at this time of year sandwiched between a score of dun and steely-grey ones.

At daybreak the sun, a flat red disc, reflected itself upon the thin white ice of the Hermit's Pool. The clustering trees, dark and icy still stood sharply against a copper sky. Underfoot the herbage was crisp and springy to the tread, every separate blade and leaf encrusted and edged with filigree frost-work. A great hush was upon everything. The trees, lately so strained and tossed with tempest, were still; even the pines, never wholly silent, had subsided to a murmur.

Flora Thompson, *The Peverell Papers*
Oxfordshire

THERE IS A beautiful, sloping acre, not far from Oxford, which a number of great elms divide into aisles and nave, while at one end a curving hawthorn and maple hedge completes them with an apse. Towards Oxford, the space is almost shut in by remote elms. On one side I hear the soft and sibilant fall of soaking grass before the scythe. The rain and sun alternating are like two lovers in dialogue; the rain smiles from the hills when the sun shines, and the sun also while the rain is falling. When the rain is not over and the sun has interrupted, the nightingale sings, where the stitchwort is starry amidst long grass that bathes the sweeping branches of thorn and brier; and I am now stabbed, and now caressed, by its changing song. Through the elms on either side, hot, rank grasses rise, crowned with a vapour of parsley flowers. A white steam from the soil faintly mists the grass at intervals. The grass and elms seem to be suffering in the rain, suffering for their quietness and solitude, to be longing for something, as perhaps Eden also dropped 'some natural tears' when left a void. A potent, warm, and not quite soothing perfume creeps over the grass, and makes the May blossom something elvish. I turn and look east. Almost at once, all these things are happily composed into one pleasant sense, and are but a frame to a tower and three spires of Oxford, like clouds – but the sky is suddenly cloudless.

Edward Thomas, *Oxford*

I NOTICED IN the poplar above me two sorts of sound: the leaves pattering and rustling against one another, each with its separate chatter; and then as accompaniment and continuous ground-tone, the wind itself breathing audibly and caressingly between leaves and round twigs and limbs.

George Sturt, *Memoirs of a Surrey Labourer*

ON THE PLAIN, and there only, can the construction – but that is too little vital a word; I should rather say the organism – the unity, the design of the sky be understood. The light wind that has been moving all night is seen to have not worked at random. It has shepherded some small flocks of cloud afield and folded others. There's husbandry in heaven. And the order has, or seems to have, the sun for its midst. Not a line, not a curve, but confesses its membership in a design declared from horizon to horizon.

Alice Meynell, *The Rhythm of Life*
Suffolk

SPRING BROUGHT THE leggy lambs running up to their mothers for short and urgent sucking sessions . . . Autumn brought the fluttering leaves, piled by the winds into the banks of confetti to jump and roll in and scatter back to the winds.

Winter seeped through our boots, aggravated our itching chilblains, but they were soon forgotten in the snowball pelting with our 'enemies'. Icicles made lovely lollyices to suck, but summer mornings were the best of all, mornings to recapture when I listen now to the evocative genius of Beethoven's 'Pastoral' Symphony, taking me back to the well-springs of my childhood, to fetching water from the well.

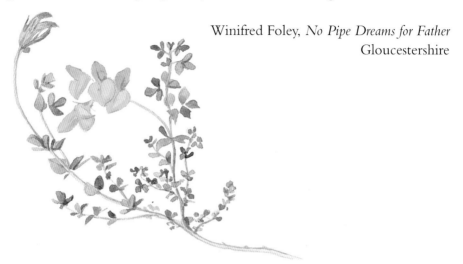

Winifred Foley, *No Pipe Dreams for Father*
Gloucestershire

A FRIEND OF the writer was once overtaken by a violent thunderstorm when alone on the heights of Cheviot. Being of a philosophical turn of mind, he quietly descended from the crest of the hill, and lying prone amongst the heather for safety, viewed the storm in all its terrific grandeur around and beneath him with no small enjoyment, but at the penalty of being thoroughly soaked by the deluge of rain. This he soon remedied so soon as the storm was over, by stripping off his clothes, sitting patiently half clad until they were somewhat dried in the scalding sunshine.

David 'Dippie' Dixon, *Upper Coquetdale*
Northumberland

DOWN HERE THE rain has been as welcome as it is to the dwellers in the south, who look for 'the rains in their due season, the first rain and the latter rain, that they may gather in their corn, their wine and their oil.' We, too have had a wet month. Old grey-headed men rub their hands and say it is a 'wunnerful rine', and that they have not known its like these seven years. Younger labourers have come home soaked from the fields, but no word of complaint has escaped them in my hearing; lads tramp up and down the roads completely indifferent to the worst the weather can do.

The cause for this rejoicing, or indifference, is not far to seek. We are in a very dry district, one to which the rain comes all too seldom; the heavy land gets hot, the crops fail, the springs run dry in the summer. At the best, we have a water-famine; at the worst, there is an outbreak of fever. Perhaps the neglect of arboriculture is the prime cause of drought, for where trees are cut down recklessly, and the beds of rivers are choked up, rainfall is always reduced, and the land suffers. Down here, where the farmers have ruled with almost feudal despotism for so long, the country has not been handled with too much intelligence. Now that a little rain has come to our assistance, nourishing the fields and feeding the springs, we are all well pleased.

S. L. Bensusan, *A Countryside Chronicle*
Essex

ON SUNDAY, 6 MAY 1906, thunder-clouds began to gather in late afternoon and rain fell heavily as thunder rolled in the distance. Then it seemed the worst was over, so brave folk ventured out to evening service, but it was not long before such a storm, as none had before known, was raging. The hill became a river and the

stream at the bottom of the village rose so high that it flooded the bridge, laying flat the walls on either side. The road was absolutely impassable there, especially after darkness had fallen, and it was only possible to see what was happening by the flashes of lightning. People whose houses were only a few yards distant daren't attempt to cross the bridge until a young farmer on horseback, returning from courting at a farm a few miles away, risked his life and proved that the road still held.

A small rick of hay was lifted bodily from the front of a riverside cottage, carried across the road by the flood, and deposited by the hedge on the far side of a field opposite. That cottage had water to within two inches of the ceiling downstairs.

Dora Trowbridge, *Somerset Remembers*

RAIN, RAIN, RAIN: the little flagged path outside my window is a streaming way, where the coming raindrops meet again the grey clouds whose storehouse they have but just now left. The grass grows greener as I watch it, the burnt patches fade, a thousand thirsty heads are uplifted for the cooling draught.

The great thrush that robs the raspberry canes is busy; yesterday he had little but dust for his guerdon, but now fresh, juicy fruit repays him as he swings to and fro on the pliant branches. The blackbirds and starlings find the worms an easy prey – poor brother worm ever ready for sacrifice. I can hear the soft expectant chatter of the family of martins under the roof; there will be good hunting, and they know it, for the flies are out when the rain is over, and there are clamorous mouths awaiting.

Michael Fairless, *The Roadmender*

ON A MORNING early in May it was raining, quietly, luxuriously, with a continuous soothing shattering-down of warm drops. In the doorway of the little toolshed I stood listening – listening to the gentle murmur on the roof, on the long fresh grass of a small orchard plot, and on the young leaves of the plum and the blossoming apple which made the daylight greener by half veiling the sky.

Beside and beyond these trees were lilacs, purpling for bloom, small hazels, young elms in a hedgerow – all fair with new greenness; and farther on, glimpses of cottage roof against the newly dug garden-ground of the steep hillside. Above the half-diaphanous green tracery of trees, cool delicious cloud, 'dropping fatness', darkened where it sagged nearer to the earth. The light was nowhere strong, but all tempered moistly, tenderly, to the tenderness of the young greenery.

I ought to have been busy, yet I stood and listened; for the earth seemed busy too, but in a softened way, managing its many businesses beautifully. The air seemed melting into numberless liquid sounds. Quite near – not three trees off – there was a nightingale nonchalantly babbling; from the neighbourhood of the cottage came, penetrating, the bleating of a newly born goat; while in the orchard just before me Bettesworth stooped over a zinc pail, which, as he scrubbed it, gave out a low metallic note. Then there were three undertones or backgrounds of sound, that of the soft-falling rain being one of them. Another, which diapered the rain-noise just as the young leaves showered their diaper-work against the clouds, was the all-but-unnoticed singing of larks, high up in the wet. Lastly, to give the final note of mellowness, of flavoured richness to the morning, I could hear through the distance which globed and softened it a frequent 'Cuckoo, cuckoo'. The sound came and died away, as if the rain had dissolved it, and came again, and again was lost.

George Sturt, *Memoirs of a Surrey Labourer*

IN THOSE DAYS it was not an effort to walk and climb hills. It was a pleasure that we really enjoyed. Of course there were sometimes mishaps! Once, myself and a friend were caught on a Sunday morning on the Tors, in a violent thunderstorm. The refreshment room was packed full with people like sardines in a tin. We could not even squeeze in. It was just before the First World War and I had on a dress made of some new kind of material. It must have been one of the first man-made materials, called, I believe, 'elephant crêpe'. I got drenched with the rain, which was really torrential, and was ashamed to walk home. Everyone looked at me. My dress had suddenly shrunk quite a way above my knees! I felt awful.

Lilian Wilson, *Ilfracombe's Yesterdays*
Devon

WE WERE SOON in the grip of the roaring, whirling, eddying flood, rushing madly around and round unable to force its way through the narrow gorge, while probably a high tide below was not helping to mend matters. From the upper reaches of the Avon this mighty volume of waters was covering the whole of the lower portion of those once famous grazing Hams.

Can one easily erase that picture from one's memory? To the east of us was a wide sheet of angry, troubled waters, with a lately risen full moon throwing its beams through breaking clouds at times and fully displaying this wild scene.

A dense fog under the influence of the rising moon was partially dispersing, its density leaving long streaks of an ethereal mist in its wake, through which the moon made a bold bid to penetrate, partially illuminating these patches and leaving long foggy white silvery streaks of highly illuminated misty banks of a ghost-like intensity all so picturesquely floating in mid air over the surface of those indomitable waters. As the rising moon gained strength an apparently never-ending reflection from that orb radiated right across that watery turbulence whilst in the self-same direction that high grey and hoary old landmark, the venerable tower of Keynsham Church, with the rising moon behind it, was vividly silhouetted from the top of that table-land on which the town is built.

S. G. Kendall, *Farming Memoirs of a West Country Yeoman*
Somerset

IT IS IMPOSSIBLE for me to describe the havoc that has been wrought here by a storm today. The storm was on us in a moment, and bushels of the stones are still lying about, though six hours since they fell. Our place was looking very charming, but presents a picture of great desolation now ... The hailstones were blinding in their density and many as large as hens' eggs. We have more than a hundred panes of glass broken and the ruin of all my garden stuff is complete. My strawberries and peas were just in bearing, but they – and even strong stuff like rhubarb – are quite pulped. Potatoes and everything are simply cut to pieces . . . I had a very exciting experience in the midst of it all. My grass was being cut with a machine. I urged the man in charge to be quick and release the horses, but he took his time, and before he could get them free they became unmanageable, the blows of the hailstones on every part of their heads and bodies being terrific. I did my best to hold them, but at last they made a plunge, breaking the pole and hurling the man into the ditch. He came out with a nasty bruise on his head and half stunned. The tornado had carried off his hat, and the sight of the great hailstones bouncing off his head was one to be remembered. I seized a heap of grass to cover him, and dragged him off to a shelter, both of us being badly wounded. I have got a great bruise on the back of my hand as big as a half-crown, where a single stone struck me, and after I had had a bath and changed you could feel the bumps on my body through my clothing. Such storms as these can only come occasionally in a century.

Revd F. A. Adams, *The Bucks Herald,* 3 July 1897
Essex

THE PURBECK VALLEY was practically free from autumn and winter mists. At other times the Channel fogs were never far away and liable to come rolling in so swiftly that the Tyneham dwellers learned to be prepared for them at any moment.

It might be a grilling summer's day with a cloudless sky, when suddenly the scene would disappear behind a drifting curtain of white vapour, with a chilling drop of temperature. We never thought of wearing thin summer frocks except for going 'inland'. No fall of the barometer gave warning of the coming change. The glass had probably stood high for days, with all the other weather portents favourable, so that the prospects for a fête or outing seemed most promising. Then all at once a cold air crept in from the sea, followed immediately by clinging, blinding fog and the mournful lowing of the Shambles light-ship, voicing its hoarse monotonous complaint. These sea mists had the advantage of keeping the valley green and, even in the longest of dry spells, the pastures held good grazing, while lawns and garden remained fresh and bright.

Lilian Bond, *Tyneham, A Lost Heritage*
Dorset

THOSE DARK NIGHTS were detested by the farm hands, the wind was like a carving-knife and it cut their hands and cheeks till they bled. They wrapped mufflers round their necks when they crossed the fields, and Joshua wore mittens so that his fingers were free, but the wool frozen like boards, and caked with ice.

Wall-mending, milking, cattle-feeding, and watering had to go on, the cowhouses and stables were cleaned, the hens, calves, pigs, and sheep had to be fed. Turnips must be chopped, and slices of dry clean hay cut as neatly from the stack as a slice of bread from the loaf, with no slattering or waste.

Tom cut the hay, for Dan was a slatterer and Joshua's head could not stand the height of the ladder, nor was his hand steady enough to hold the cutting-knife. So Tom cut and Dan trussed the hay and carried it to the barns ready for foddering, a walking haystack as he staggered across the snowy field with only his two legs showing.

Alison Uttley, *The Country Child*
Derbyshire

THE SECONDARY RAINBOW was called the 'water-gull', and was supposed to be necessary to make the weather sign a satisfactory one. If one was seen alone, or with only an imperfect 'water-gull', it was deemed unlucky. In other parts of England (e.g. Yorkshire) it would seem that attempts were made to 'cross out', or get rid of, the bow, by making a cross on the ground. Sometimes this was done by the foot, or by taking two pieces of stick and laying them on the ground and placing a small stone at the end of each stick. Sometimes straws were similarly used, or even the crossing of the forefingers of each hand was considered quite as effectual. This charm was supposed to cause the rainbow to disappear; but one may well believe that by the time some of these charms were got ready the rainbow had disappeared of its own accord.

John Symonds Udal, Dorsetshire Folk-Lore

THERE IS SOMETHING nutty in the short autumn day – shorter than its duration as measured by hours, for the enjoyable day is between the clearing of the mist and the darkening of the shadows. The nuts are ripe, and with them is associated wine and fruit. They are hard but tasteful; if you eat one you want ten, and after ten twenty. In the wine there is a glow, a spot like tawny sunlight; it falls on your hand as you lift the glass . . .

The autumn itself is nutty, brown, hard, frosty and sweet. Nuts are hard, frosts are hard; but the one is sweet, and the other braces the strong. Exercise often wearies in the spring, and in the summer heat is scarcely to be faced; but in the autumn, to those who are well, every step is bracing and hardens the frame, as the sap is hardening in the trees.

Richard Jefferies, Nature Near London
Surrey

THEN CAME A day that was a revelation; I all at once had a deeper sense and more intimate knowledge of what summer really is to all the children of life; for it chanced that on that effulgent day even the human animal, usually regarded as outside of nature, was there to participate in the heavenly bounty . . . High up the larks were raining down their brightest, finest music; not rising skyward nor falling earthward, but singing continuously far up in that airy blue space that was their home. The little birds that live in the furze, the titlarks, whitethroats, linnets and stonechats, sprang upwards at frequent intervals and poured out their strains when on the wing. Each bird had its characteristic flight and gestures and musical notes, but all alike expressed the overflowing gladness that summer inspired, even as the flowers seemed to express it in their intense colours; and as the butterflies expressed in their fluttering dances, and in the rapturous motions of their wings when at rest. There were rabbits out, but they were not feeding, and when disturbed ran but fifteen or twenty yards away, then sat and looked at me with their big, round, prominent eyes, apparently too contented with life to suspect harm . . . I all at once came upon some children lying on the grass on the slope of a down. There were five of them, scattered about, all lying on their backs, their arms stretched crossways, straight out, their hands open. It looked as if they had instinctively spread themselves out, just as a butterfly at rest opens wide its wings to catch the beams. The hot sun shone full on their fresh young faces; and though wide awake they lay perfectly still as I came up and walked slowly past them, looking from upturned face to face, each expressing perfect contentment; and as I successively caught their eyes they smiled, though still keeping motionless and silent as the bunnies that had regarded me a while before, albeit without smiling, Brer Rabbit being a serious little beast. Their quietude and composure in the presence of a stranger was unusual, and like the confidence of the wild rabbits on that day was caused by the delicious sensation of summer in the blood. We in our early years are little wild animals, and the wild animals are little children.

W. H. Hudson, *Nature in Downland*
Sussex

TRADITION AND SUPERSTITION

There is an old superstition concerning the cuckoo's cry in the South of England. If when you hear the cuckoo, you begin to run and count the cuckoo's cry's, and continue running until out of ear-shot, you will add as many years to your life as you count calls; – at least so the old women tell you in Devonshire.

Edith Holden, *The Country Diary of an Edwardian Lady*

The folk-memory of a community is a powerful thing. The countryman, working close to the earth, is aware of its mysteries and its magic. A farmer might plough, sow and harvest, but there were unseen deities that governed the success or otherwise of his efforts. So local legends would grow, surrounding certain places and events with deep significance, aided by an oral tradition of storytelling that was as creative as it was vivid. The dark landscape of a pre-electric village or the lights thrown by the flicker of a smithy fire – a smith was regarded as someone who held strange powers – were powerful stimuli to the rural imagination, just as the echo of a footstep on a country lane would haunt the lonely traveller as it rang back from the darkness of the nocturnal woodland.

The church was there, of course, but pagan superstition had been there longer, and its shadows continued to stretch across the landscape. Even the wildlife – so much a part of everyday life – became a part of the supernatural ordering of things; an insect behaving in an uncharacteristic way could be full of awful portents. Even the lighter celebrations – the seasonal festivals that marked the movement of the year, May Day for example – held the distant rumour of half-forgotten rites that belonged to a pre-Christian countryside.

It is hardly surprising that a land such as Britain should contain such a rich blend of darkness and light in its culture. This is, after all, a country of many peoples, and each has provided germs of lore that grew over the centuries in the rural landscape. The crackle of a winter fire was a powerful accompaniment to stories – always verified by a knowing nod – of the phantoms of the countryside, or of tiny silver beings, dancing in a dewy ring on a moonlit summer's night.

THE OLD COUNTRYMAN is made wise by the wisdom of the earth. His daily contact with the principles of growth, his continuous traffic with the seasons, may leave him subject to superstitions; but superstition itself is an acknowledgement that there is a mystic Something behind phenomena.

Sir William Beach Thomas, *A Countryman's Creed*
Cumbria

'I A SIN they little people as dances about in the moonlight.'

'Where was that?'

'At eethrup down an the lawn. Some yeeurs agoo I was night watchman down at eethrup House, and ivvery night from twelve o'clock to one in the marnin I had to be at the pavilion. I alwiz had a good big dog wi me in ceeas e met any porchers ur see anybody a-prowlin about. I hadn't bin thaiur very long when one night as the moo was gettin an tords full, and I was a-standin under some laurels so that nobody could see me, I heeurd sich a rustlin about in the leeavs. I took no no-atice an it as e thought twas only a lot of rabbuts a-scampering about, but th' ole dog kept an a-growlin and tuggin at his chee-an. At last I meead him kaip quiet, but it waunt fur long as he started agen, and would kaip an, so e thought e ood have a look to see what the row was about. I went up to the edge uv the bush and looked wheeur the noise was a-comin frum, and begoy! what e thought was rabbuts was little men, the funniest lookin little cocks as ivver I did see. I dinno what to meeak an em, I could hardly belaive mi own eyes. I nivver did see sich gooins-an. They were all an a opun speeace an the ground wheeur the moonlight shone through the trais. I could see ivvery one an em fur ivver so long, and they nivver took a bit a noatice a me ur mi dog, though some an em come quite neeur the bush. They danced and jumped and cee-aperd all round the pleeace and pulled sich funny feeaces as I coont kaip mi eyes awf em.'

H. Harman, *Sketches of the Bucks Countryside*

OLIVER CROMWELL'S MEMORY is still very much respected among the labouring folk. Every possible work is attributed to his hand, and even the names of places are set down to his inventive genius. Thus they tell you that when he passed through Aldsworth he did not think much of the village (it is certainly a very dull little place), so he snapped his fingers and exclaimed, 'That's all 'e's worth!'. On arriving at Ready Token, where was an ancient inn, he found it full of guests; he therefore exclaimed, 'It's already taken!' Was ever such nonsense heard? Yet these good folk believe every tradition of this kind, and delight in telling you such stories . . . One of the chief traditions of this locality, and one that doubtless has more truth in it than most of the stories the natives tell you, relates that two hundred years ago people were frequently murdered at Ready Token Inn when returning with their pockets full of money from the big fairs at Gloucester and Oxford. A labouring friend of mine was telling me the other day of the wonderful disappearance of a packman and a 'jewelrer', as he called him. For many years nothing was heard of them, but about twenty years ago some 'skellingtons' were dug up on the exact spot where the inn stood, so their disappearance was accounted for.

This same man told me the following story about the origin of Hangman's Stone, near Northleach:

'A man stole a "ship" [sheep], and carried it tied to his neck and shoulders by a rope. Feeling rather tired, he put the "ship" down on top of the "stwun" [stone] to rest a bit; but suddenly it rolled off the other side, and hung him – broke his neck.'

Hangman's Stone may be seen to this day.

J. Arthur Gibbs, *A Cotswold Village*
Gloucestershire

WHEN THE LAST of summer had given place to the fullness of late November, when fogs were prevalent and the darkness each evening was of a kind that made it easier to tread the village ways by their feel underfoot rather than by any attempt at sight; then, as for centuries before, on the twenty-fourth day of the month, a company of youths performed the traditional fight of King George with the Turkish Knight.

They repeated those stereotypical phrases and performed every separate act of the drama as strictly as if it had been a religious duty, as their fathers had done before them; and in neither did they attempt the slightest deviation of speech or gesture. No script of the play existed; the old men of the village knew every word and act to the last letter; they had performed the play themselves when they were young, and would not have tolerated anything different, no matter how much of an improvement it may have been from a dramatic standpoint.

The Mummers' performance was undoubtedly a notable unchanged survival of very ancient rural life, coming down from a past altogether too remote for anything

definite of its origin to be known. Yet the sudden flinging open of the door, and the announced entry, with the subsequent fight that needed ample space to be properly rendered, immediately suggest a far ruder order of life: the common homestead in some forest clearing, where on the dark winter evening such a visit from a neighbouring settlement would be cheerfully welcome.

Walter Rose, *Good Neighbours*
Buckinghamshire

THE POACHER CREPT from the darkness into the glaring smithy light; for in country parts the anvil might sometimes be heard clanging at all hours of the night. As a rule, every face was blackened; and it was this, I suppose, rather than the fact that dark nights were chosen, that gave the gangs the name of black-fishers ... The country folk of those days were more superstitious than they are now, and it did not take much to turn the black-fishers back. There was not a barn or byre in the district that had not its horseshoe over the door. Another popular device for frightening away witches and fairies was to hang bunches of garlic about the farms. I have known a black-fishing expedition stopped because a 'yellow-yite', or yellow-hammer, hovered round the gang when they were setting out. Still more ominous was the 'peat' when it appeared with one or three companions. An old rhyme about this bird runs: 'One is joy, two is grief, three's a bridal, four is death.' Such snatches of superstition are still to be heard amidst the gossip of a north-country smithy.

J. M. Barrie, *Auld Licht Idylls*
Angus (Tayside)

HEARD TODAY AN old country tradition: that if a woman goes off her own premises before being churched, e.g. crosses a road that forms the boundary of her residence, she may be made to do penance or be excommunicated. I cannot explain this, but it reminds me of what old Mr Hibbs of Bere Regis told me lately: that a native of that place, now ninety, says he remembers a young woman doing penance in Bere Church for singing scandalous songs about 'a great lady'. The girl stood in a white sheet while she went through 'the service of penance', whatever that was.

Thomas Hardy, *The Life of Thomas Hardy*
Dorset

AN OLD PARISH clerk and sexton living at the foot of the churchyard, the garden of whose cottage was only divided from it by a low wall, was wont to be much annoyed by a poor half-witted girl of the village repairing to the church porch night after night and disturbing his rest by singing psalms. With the intention of frightening away the intruder he, one moonlight night, wrapped himself in a sheet, and walking round the church came upon the girl as usual singing in the porch. Instead of being alarmed, however, at the unexpected apparition as had been fully counted upon, she addressed the supposed spirit as follows: 'Here's a soul coming! Whose soul be you? Be you my granfer's or granmer's, or –' (naming somebody who had recently been buried there). Then, after a pause, and looking round, she continued, 'H'm! souls *be* about tonight! For there's a black 'un, too, and he's trying to come up to the whit' 'un; an' he's coming on so fast that if the whit' 'un don't take care the black 'un 'll catch en.' Upon hearing these words, the sexton, who had anticipated the flight and terror of the poor girl on his making his appearance, now felt the effects of that terror recoiling on himself; and, looking upon it as a judgement for his cruel conduct, took to his heels with all possible speed. Upon seeing this, the girl, clapping her hands to encourage him to the utmost, exclaimed: 'Run, whit' soul; black soul'll catch 'ee! Run, whit' soul, black soul'll catch 'ee!' and repeated this several times with the greatest fervency. The sexton, now becoming perfectly wild with fear on hearing these words, glanced hastily behind him, and fancying he saw a dark figure close to his heels (which was probably that of his own shadow in the moonlight) tore down the path and over the low wall into his garden, never stopping till he was safe inside his own door. From the effects of this shock a serious illness followed, and, as the legend goeth, he 'peeled' from head to foot. It is needless to add that the girl remained unmolested for the future.

John Symonds Udal, *Dorsetshire Folk-Lore*

OUR HOUSE OVERLOOKED the churchyard and we often had to walk through this, past some of the old gravestones, on our way home. What a golden opportunity for a country boy, who was used to the dark (I can't remember street lights for many years), to creep up behind Auntie Cis, scaring her so much that she would run home as fast as her legs could carry her. Her bedroom faced the church and on moonlit nights, I would get her to look out over the churchyard and would make all kinds of silly remarks – 'Look, that gravestone moved! Look at that grave' (one with an uneven mound), 'that chap's got his knees up . . .'

D. A. Judd, *Living in the Country*
Northamptonshire

AT BRADWELL, IN the Peak of Derbyshire, once lived a man known as Master John, who was reported to be a wise man, and whose advice was sought by all the people in the village. It is said that the ghost of a child who had been murdered in the village could not be appeased, and so the aid of Master John was invoked. Master John pronounced the words 'In the name of the Father, Son, and Holy Ghost, why troublest thou me?' and turned the ghost of the child into a large fish. This fish used to appear, it is said, at a place called the Lum Mouth, and also at Lumley Pool, in Bradwell, on Christmas Day to people who fetched water from the wells there. When anybody saw the ghost in the form of a fish he would run away screaming 'the fish, the fish'.

S. O. Addy, *Household Tales with Other Traditional Remains*

MAY DAY WERE kept in our village, but not like it is in most places. We di'n't have no May Queen, and we di'n't go gathering may 'cos there wern't no may to gather right down in the fen, though if we'd a-wanted to gather it, no doubt we should a-took the trouble to go to Biggin Fields, where there were plenty. All we had a-May Day were a sort o' May garland. It were in the form of a doll, an old rag doll. A couple o' tall posts were set up, one each side o' the high way, with a clothes line stretched tight between them. Then the May doll were pegged on the line, over the middle o' the road. Our mothers spent hours making us little sawdust balls to pelt at the dolly, to see if we could turn it over the line. Old women who kept shops did a good trade in these sawdust balls at halfpenny a time, in the evenings when the

young men and women who had a few pennies they'd saved for the occasion come in to join in the fun. Then the doll on the line only served to get the crowd together, and it wer'n't long afore they'd forgot all about her and started playing the usual games like long tag and round tag and 'Fox and Hares' and 'Kiss-in-the-Ring' which were really what they'd come for. But by that time the little ones had been took home to bed.

Kate Mary Edwards: Sybil Marshall, *Fenland Chronicle*
Huntingdonshire

ON THE LAST morning of April the children would come to school with bunches, baskets, arms and pinafores full of flowers – every blossom they could find in the fields and hedges or beg from parents and neighbours. On the previous Sunday some of the bigger boys would have walked six or eight miles to a distant wood where primroses grew. These, with violets from the hedgerows, cowslips from the meadows, and wallflowers, oxlips and sprays of pale red flowering currant from the cottage gardens, formed the main supply. A sweetbriar hedge in the schoolmistress's garden furnished unlimited greenery.

Piled on desks, table and floor, this supply appeared inexhaustible, but the garland was large, and as the work of dressing it proceeded, it soon became plain that the present stock wouldn't 'hardly go nowheres', as the children said. So foraging parties were sent out, one to the Rectory, another to Squire's, and others to outlying farmhouses and cottages . . . Then the Top-Knot, consisting of a bunch of crown imperial, yellow and brown, was added to crown the whole, and the fragrant, bowering structure was sprinkled with water and set aside for the night.

While the garland was being dressed, an older girl, perhaps the May Queen herself, would be busy in a corner making the crown. This always had to be a daisy crown; but, meadow daisies being considered too common and also possessing insufficient staying power, garden daisies, white and red, were used, with a background of dark, glossy, evergreen leaves . . . The final touches were given to the garland when the children assembled at six o'clock on May Day morning. Then a large china doll in a blue frock was brought forth from the depths of the school needlework chest and arranged in a sitting position on a little ledge in the centre front of the garland. This doll was known as 'the lady', and a doll of some kind was considered essential. Even in those parishes where the garland had degenerated into a shabby nosegay carried aloft at the top of a stick, some dollish image was mixed in with the flowers. The

attitude of the children to the lady is interesting. It was understood that the garland was her garland, carried in her honour. The lady must never be roughly handled. If the garland turned turtle, as it was apt to do later in the day, when the road was rough and the bearers were grown weary, the first question was always, 'Is the lady all right?' (Is it possible that the lady was once 'Our Lady', she having in her turn, perhaps, replaced an earlier effigy of some pagan spirit of the newly decked earth?)

Flora Thompson, *Lark Rise to Candleford*
Oxfordshire

THERE WERE ANOTHER spot, along the high road to St Mary's that had a haunt. At one particular place, a white cat 'ould come out across the dyke on one side o' the road, and cross it, a bit squywannick, right in front o' the feet of any late travellers, and go down into the dyke on the other side. The finny thing was that it di'n't matter how long you looked for 'er once she'd gone down over the dykeside, you could never find her. Scores o' people 'ave seen 'er, but whether she were just a ordinary flesh and blood cat wi' very reg'lar habits, or a feline ghost, is never been proved as I know on. Once, when I were young, I were coming down the road with a gang of other young fellows. Me and Bill ... were very scornful about it, and Bill said 'If the b— shows itself tonight I'll prove as it ain't no sperrit: I'll kelp it into the drain on the toe o' my boot.' So on we went, and at the very identical spot, out come pussy, across the road no mor'n a foot in front of our feet. I don't know how the others felt, but my hair rose up and very near pushed my cap off. I see Bill lift 'is foot up, and it seemed to me as if the ol' cat lingered about deliberately, right in front on 'im; then she turned 'er 'ead, and looked straight at 'im, an' 'is foot wavered about a bit, and then 'e put it down again. Puss slunk off across the road, an' over the side o' the dyke she went, just like she allus did.

Soon as she'd gone out o' sight, I felt better, and tried to pretend I ha'n't bin frit at all. 'Well,' I said to Bill, 'why di'n't you give it one?'

'Bill,' 'e answered, 'Bill, I daresn't. I were afraid as me fut 'oulkd goo right through it.'

William Henry Edwards: Sybil Marshall, *Fenland Chronicle,*
Huntingdonshire

CARADOC IS THE finest isolated hill in Shropshire, bolder as well as higher than the Wrekin. Popularly known as Querdoc it has played its part in the folklore as well as in the rural festivities of the county, for when legendary events have provided a suitable occasion it has risen to it and burst into a volcano, and the caves where Caractacus hid after his defeats are still obvious on its steep face. Wakes were very important functions in Shropshire till the middle of the last century, and some of them were held on hilltops, notably on those of Caradoc and the Wrekin. The former associated itself since remote times with Trinity Sunday. Barrels of ale were then broached, refreshment booths erected, hawkers went to and fro, and rough sports, notably wrestling, were engaged in, and much fiddling and dancing, with other evidences of old-world heartiness . . . The Wrekin wake, held on the first Sunday in May, was renowned for the annual fight between the mining and the agricultural interest, which became at last so bloodthirsty that the feast was abolished. The tradition, however, has by no means died out, for young people, I am told, still repair, though in demurer and more peaceful mood, both to Caradoc and the Wrekin on the old fête days, and make love no doubt in board school English.

A.G. Bradley, *In the March and Borderland of Wales*

ALTHOUGH THERE ARE now very few, if any, superstitious beliefs connected with Midsummer fires on St John's Eve, they appear to be survivals of the pagan rite in honour of the god Baal. Some of the practices which used to be carried out in England were certain very similar to those of the worshippers of Baal and Moloch. But . . . if the Midsummer fires are of pagan origin, they are at present lit with no other design than that of continuing an old custom.

Till comparatively recent times a bonfire was lit on St John's Eve in several Northumbrian villages, and is still at Whaton, which, remote from rail and tramway, retains most of its old customs. There the fire has never been omitted within the memory of the oldest inhabitant . . .

As Midsummer approaches much wood is marked out for the bonfire, sometimes with the consent of local farmers. When this has been cut, it is brought into the village with a certain amount of formality . . . While the building is in progress a remarkable scene takes place. Of a sudden every house empties, all the villagers turning out with one accord. Old men and women, middle-aged couples, youths and maidens, school lads and lasses, toddlers in short frocks – the whole populace appears; and presently groups are gathered everywhere to watch the stacking of the bonfire.

Later on the children, joining hands, form a moving ring round the pile, and dance till they are tired. They are keenly interested in the ceremony, because they always have a scramble for sweets, which are scattered for their special enjoyment. Youths and maidens also dance in the neighbourhood of the pile, a fiddler or other instrumentalist providing the music.

As darkness creeps over the countryside, and the shades of night blot out familiar details, there is a cry of 'Light her!' . . . A moment later a flame leaps skywards, to be joined by another, and then another, till at last the whole village is illuminated. The Baal fire burns!

Beyond dancing, there is no subsequent festivity or ceremony. But, if local tradition may be trusted, there used to be some superstitious practices. People jumped over the fire and through it. In bygone times, too, stealthy appropriation of ashes was not uncommon. Both these circumstances point in the same direction – to the remarkably long continuance of ancient rites and uses of fire.

Michael MacDonagh,
Sir Benjamin Stone's Pictures: Festivals, Ceremonies and Customs
Northumbria

THAT ABOUT the young woman he had spoken of is a queer little story in this enlightened land. She was apparently in very good health, a wife, and the mother of a small child; but a few weeks before her sudden death a strange thing occurred to trouble her mind. One afternoon, when sitting alone in her cottage taking tea, she saw a cricket come in at the open door, and run straight into the middle of the room. There it remained motionless and without stirring from her seat she took a few moist tea-leaves and threw them down near the welcome guest. The cricket moved up to the leaves, and when it touched them and appeared just about to begin sucking their moisture, to her dismay it turned aside, ran away out at the door, and disappeared. She informed all her neighbours of this startling occurrence, and sadly spoke of an aunt who was living at another village and was known to be in bad health. 'It must be for her,' she said; 'we'll soon be hearing bad news of her, I'm thinking.' But no bad news came, and when she was beginning to believe that the strange cricket that had refused to remain in the house had proved a false prophet, the warning of the owl came to startle her afresh. At noonday she heard it hooting in the great horse chestnut overgrown with ivy that stands at the roadside, close to her cottage. The incident was discussed by the villagers with their usual solemnity and head-shakings, and now the young woman gave up all hopes of her sick aunt's recovery; for that one of her people was going to die was certain, and it would be no other than that ailing one. And, after all, the message and warning was for her and not the aunt. Not many days after the owl had hooted in broad daylight, she dropped down dead in her cottage while engaged in some domestic work.

W. H. Hudson, *Birds and Man*
Herefordshire

Youth
AND AGE

May 12th ... Had an endless tramp over the bog after the ponies ... One tiny mouse-coloured foal about a week old kept running in circles round and round its mother and skipping in the air like a lamb.

Edith Holden, *The Nature Notes of an Edwardian Lady*

Recollections of childhood sharpen as we grow older, and the memories gathered here are made more poignant by the fact that they belong to an age that was on the edge of great change, a time when it was becoming clear that a way of life was about to vanish for ever. It is this that makes the years around 1900 seem so strangely distant to us today. Thomas Hardy, for instance, was born into a world where little had changed for centuries: yet he lived to see the birth of the car, radio, cinema – and world war.

Just as the act of looking back will recall schooldays and the games and pastimes of youth, so does it provide images of those who inhabited that time, an older generation still, taking us beyond the realms of living memory into what we have come to call history. So this so-called 'distant' world becomes suddenly very close. Dame Barbara Cartland recalls songs that to her mother meant memories of the Boer War; the overlapping of generations created a handing-on of stories and recollections in which an apparently unchanging past was kept alive, the past overshadowing the present in a way we have forgotten today. After all, a country person of eighty, living in 1900, would have had access to a previous generation's community memory that would take them back as far as the middle of the eighteenth century.

I WAS BORN on 4 July 1912 in a farm cottage at Chalk, Kent, the youngest of four sons. My birth was celebrated by my father with one of his friends singing to the accompaniment of a melodeon, seated in front of the cowshed opposite our cottage. I learned later that the melodeon was the only form of entertainment we had in those days.

L. Wallis, *To be a Farmer's Boy*

MY EARLIEST MEMORY – I can't have been more than three – is of sitting alone on the grass, gazing through a doorway into the stable yard. I looked up and thought I saw my father nailed to the door. I remember screaming and shouting up to the nursery and the nanny screaming down, 'Joe! Joe! Is the master hanging on the stable door?' It was my father's hunting breeches which some stable lad had hung up to scrub. I remember it so clearly and no one can have told me. I can also remember being chased across the yard by two hound puppies before two stable lads came to save me. It was rather like being hunted by wolves.

Molly Keane, *Country Living*
County Kildare

AFTER WE HAD all been to church to the family service – at which we would be disappointed if we did not sing 'Hark the Herald Angels Sing!' and 'The First Nowell' – we would hurry home to start opening our presents, some of which had been collected during the year . . . As a child I drew pictures, and painted shells and other things to give them as presents, too. One of the things I did was to write my first book as a present for my mother at Christmas. It was called *The Little Slide-maker*. I also illustrated it, and I have it still. It has been on show on various occasions. It is not a very artistic effort but I think I was five when I first started it . . .

I remember a particular little ceremony in the evening, which to us was the climax of a lovely Christmas. After dinner we sat round the fireside and started by singing songs that my mother loved as a girl and which were part of her history.

'Goodbye Dolly, I Must Leave You' was the popular tune when she was young and all her young men went off to fight in the Boer War. 'You Are My Honey-Honeysuckle, I Am the Bee' was popular at the time she fell in love with my father and they got married. It is perhaps the reason why I am so keen on honey!

Many other beautiful old melodies brought back to her times that were happy or sad but are now nostalgic and precious memories.

Dame Barbara Cartland, *Country Living*
Gloucestershire

TO US CHILDREN our Dad was the fount of wisdom, kindliness and honour. Whenever we wanted his attention he became a child among us – slow, dreamy and always understanding. He never minded being woken up at any odd hour to help with a fretful baby, or to nurse a sick child. Once, when I had earache in the small hours, he took me, sobbing with pain, downstairs; he made up a good fire, warmed a brick in the oven to hold up to my head to try and ease the pain, cuddled me on his lap and tried to distract me with the tales of Brer Rabbit, all to no avail. His blackened, beloved old pipe, charred with the residue of strong tobacco, was the balm and cure for all his own pains, and at last in desperation, he gave it to me.

'There, my wench, thee have a few puffs o'feyther's bacca – that'll take the pain away.'

And so it must have, for I awoke in bed, late the next morning, with my earache gone.

Winifred Foley, *A Child in the Forest*
Gloucestershire

I THINK THERE were only about five marbles between the whole school, and we used to try to win them with buttons. A marble would be put in a scooped-out hollow in the ground and we would throw a pebble at it. The one who got the nearest pebble to the marble would be paid in buttons by the rest in the game. Then he would have to kneel down and throw all the buttons together and if they all landed in the hole the winner got the marble. We used to get a jolly good hiding at home when our mothers found the buttons had been cut off her coat. If you had a marble in your pocket the whack on your backside didn't bother you none – but if you had just lost a precious marble then by-hyes 'twould make your eyes sting!

Henry Curtis: June Lewis, *The Village School*
Gloucestershire

I WAS PLEASED when choir practice night came. We put a bit of overtime in at play after practice. When asked 'Why are you late?' I knew the answers all right. The games we played at night were 'Kick can awallop', 'Mike, mike strike a light there are smugglers on the shore.' . . . In the winter games we played by day were hoop trundling, marbles, five stones, toad in the hole, football and cricket and played around the old water mill at Michelham Priory.

Gaius Carley, *The Memoirs of Gaius Carley*
Sussex

I WENT TO the village school when I was four and a half years old, staying there until I was fourteen whilst they tried to teach me the three Rs. I have few recollections of those early schooldays but I do remember that I used to repeat everything parrot-fashion following exactly what I believed the other children were saying. We used to say Grace and it was not until I could read that I found that my oft-repeated 'The Plague of Flies sent down from heaven' should have been 'The bread of Life sent down from heaven'. I am sure that many others made similar errors through repeating misheard words. Before I left the village school my sister became a pupil teacher there.

Betty Rutterford, *A Wheelwright of Hoxne*
Suffolk

THE SCHOOLS OF the period varied. The free ones in the town, usually gaunt grey buildings with high windows out of which no child could see, were dark and dreary. They were divided into three sections and over their separate entrances were the words 'Boys', 'Girls' or 'Infants'.

The village schools, often having lady teachers only, were very different. Discipline was not so rigid and punishments apparently not so severe; though in schools of every type the cane seemed to be used, often unnecessarily we may now think. The country schools were often led by dedicated women who, because of the smaller number of the children, were able to know and love (and therefore to help) their pupils. Good morals were taught and practised and many adults have testified to their appreciation of these early teachers. Village children at that time were as poor as their town counterparts, but it was not so evident. Although in some cases it was tyrannical, the overlordship of the Manor and of the Church was mostly benevolent; and this had its effect in the schools.

Jessie M. Stonham, *Daughter of Wyedean and Kernow*
Herefordshire

I WAS BORN 28 January 1900 and started school in a good church school built in the 1860s on my fifth birthday and left on my thirteenth. The school had a headmistress and two assistant teachers and an average of one hundred pupils. It was kept reasonably warm and there was no modern sanitation, and nowhere to wash your hands . . . We had a slate to learn to write on and we worked in a smaller room for two or three years, and the ones that done the best work had to march in step to show the headmistress with our slates held high in front of us. We got a smirk from her and a pat on the head or back. When we were older and in her class if we didn't do the work quite so good she used to come behind us as we sat at our desks and dig us in the ribs or crump us on the knuckles with her pointer. Yes, they were quite lavish with the punishments. You had to hold out your hand and two or three stinging strokes with a thin cane. I didn't tell my mother or she would have said you must have deserved it, and many times since I'm glad she let me take it.

> Fred Gambie, *To be a Farmer's Boy*
> Cambridgeshire

WE HAD TWO rooms, a large one for the bigger kids and a small one for the infants. We had long desks so you sat in rows and scratched away on the old slates – and spat on them to clean them. There were a hundred or so of us in the school altogether, although they weren't usually all in at the same time. Like harvest time – they were away helping their parents in the fields, or potato-sowing or hop-picking. Or races, Battle Fair, bonfire time and Guy Fawkes. On 7 July 1893, the wedding day of the Duke of York, we all had a holiday. And of course they used to close the school down regularly for measles or influenza.

Then in the winter you'd get some away if it was raining and storming, or snowing – and, by Christ, we got some snow, over the top of the hedges sometimes. A mother might keep her child at home if it hadn't got a good pair of well dubbined boots or a warm coat. And even if it did have, it couldn't always get them dry in front of the schoolroom stove: we had those old tortoise stoves with an iron smoke-pipe. Of course in the summer it was so hot and stuffy you couldn't breathe. I reckon the old germs loved it in there.

There were no school meals and no water taps. We had to take our own lunches in with us and some kids from big families would carry in a sack of food every day and a bottle of cold tea. Well, they needed it because some of the boys were great big things; by the time they were thirteen or fourteen they were men.

When school was over most of us played in a big field in the village; you'd call it a park now. We played cricket there, and marbles and spinning tops – the old box-tops. In the summer we used to go swimming. There were two ponds over at my aunt's place and we called them Broomham Ponds. No swimming trunks or nothing, just as you were born.

Gilbert Sargent: Dave Arthur, *A Sussex Life*

WHEN WE GOT into school we had prayers, and then set down to the morning's work. There were no playtime or 'break', and even the little child'en worked through until dockey time without being allowed out. First of all we got our slates out and 'made pot-hooks' – practising our letters with a squeaking slate pencil. We used to love the job of spitting on our slates to clean them, and rubbing it off with our sleeve. I remember once when my brother had a present of a beautiful new slate and pencil, at home, and he sat drawing on it till it were full and then cleaning it in the usual way to start again. I did want to have a turn with it, but he wouldn't let me, so I set by his side and watched him enviously. Then it come to me how I could take part in his treasure, and next time his slate was full I leaned over with my mouth ready and said 'Do you want any spit?'

Kate Mary Edwards: Sybil Marshall, *Fenland Chronicle*
Huntingdonshire

WHEN I WAS nine years old I used to go to Yeovil to get the fish in a little hand cart, come back and be in school by nine o'clock. Out again at ten o'clock, go into the village with Father to sell the fish. In school again at two, out at three or three-thirty, and perhaps go to Sherborne with the fish or up round new buildings. And when I finished my round I used to come back down Bradford Abbas about nine o'clock at night. I used to go in the pub and have half a pint. Father would have a pint of cider. It was threepence for ale, tuppence for beer. And I used to enjoy it. Children were going to pubs, that time then. They didn't care who drunk beer or whatnot. Children could always have a sip of beer if they wanted to.

Harry Gillham, *The Nineties*
Dorset

IT WAS A church school. We started the morning by singing a hymn, then we had an hour's religious education by the vicar. We had four and a half miles to walk to school, wet or dry. The village, Lowick, had another school and several shops. Having older brothers I had to wear a lot of their cast-off clothing.

At Christmas it was the custom to buy the teachers a Christmas gift. One year the boys bought a goose for the man and a duck for the woman. They were both alive. When the teachers came in the morning they were both told, before they went in, that their presents were in the school, but they had to catch them first. They chased the duck and goose round the classroom while the kids watched through the windows.

Robert Fortune, *To be a Farmer's Boy*
Northumberland

THE NEAREST SCHOOL was two miles away at Hawkley, and we walked there and back every day. The school was a simple affair, run by a Mr and Mrs Hooker; Mr Hooker took the boys whilst Mrs Hooker looked after the girls. On fine afternoons Mr Hooker (whom my brother always called 'Mr Snooker') decided that fresh air was better for us than book learning, and put the lads to work weeding his garden. Meanwhile Mrs Hooker found some darning and sewing in her house to keep the girls out of mischief.

Bill Street, unpublished memoir
Hampshire

IT WAS ALWAYS safe to go to school on our own, although we were very young, and we used to play with our hoops and whips and tops and the only time we were ever taken to school was when the weather was so stormy that it wasn't safe to walk on the paths. So we walked along the middle of the road, because there wasn't any traffic, and father always went with us, to make sure we stayed there until we got safely in the school door. So we were not cut by slates blowing off the roofs.

Now the schoolchildren all had jobs after school, or before school. That was quite regular for the older children and Mr Kidd trained some of his children very well in gardening and some of them hated it at the time, but they were grateful for it afterwards.

Mary Hall, *We're the Characters Now*
Cambridgeshire

SUNDAY SCHOOL TREATS were often held at Woolacombe. They were indeed Red Letter Days for us. Sometimes they were held in a field at Ilfracombe. Killacleave was one of the favourite places . . . Farmers used to lend their long-tailed carts for the occasion, the bottoms filled with straw on which the younger children sat and were transported to whichever place was chosen. If Woolacombe, we elder ones walked to the station, then we all went off to Mortehoe Station. There the little ones would get off the train and on to a cart, but we walked to the sands. It is all downhill; we all thoroughly enjoyed it. Going back to the station, we usually swanked by riding

in a carriage – in those days many Woolacombe men earned their living by driving people to and from the station. It is over two miles and all uphill from the sands; we used to ride four in a carriage which cost two shillings – that was sixpence each. We thought we were grown up but I am afraid the poor driver got no tip from us. I expect we never gave a thought to that. I doubt if we had any more; sixpence was a lot in the early 1900s.

During our afternoon when the races were over we would walk around the corner to Barricane Beach; there we would look for shells. Very many pretty ones were to be found there. We used to stick them on to boxes or make them into necklaces.

Lilian Wilson, *Ilfracombe's Yesterdays*
Devon

ONE DAY I was given a thrashing which wasn't needed, and when the master went to put the stick away in the desk, I ran up the school and opened the door. The children called 'He's run, sir'. I got my cap and away I went, up College Hill where some bigger boys were ploughing. I walked up and down with them until dinner-time, and then I went to Mr Holloway, the blacksmith, and blew the bellows for him. He asked why I was not at school, and then I said, 'I runned oof', and that was the end of my schooling.

Anon: June Lewis, *The Village School*
Gloucestershire

IN THOSE DAYS healthy young men and maidens left cards to their elders; such energetic pastimes as country dances, 'blind man's buff' and 'hunt the slipper' accorded better with their simple active life. Their mirth though noisy was innocent, and if a kiss or two were snatched beneath the mistletoe during the hurly-burly, the offence as a rule was speedily condoned by the insulted damsel, who accepted the reasonableness of her swain's argument that it would be 'nothen but a waste for Farmer Pinmarsh to hang up that fine bough if no use weren't made on it'.

Eleanor G. Hayden, *Travels Round Our Village*
Berkshire

THE GIRLS ALL have something wifely about them. The wooer never forgets that the sweetheart may be the wife; he wishes her less care than her mother had, and looks forward to old age in her company. He is not a wild wooer. He is content to sit in a gathering and hear his Jane 'put in a good word now and then', and have a smile and a blush from her at the door on parting: having carried her pail he is satisfied to know that she would have bowed when she took it back had it not been too heavy. He wants a maid who is 'good and true', 'good and fair', and healthy, and to have always beside him the 'welcome face and homely name'. Once he may have been ruffled by a mere beauty in a scarlet cloak, but probably he soon sets his heart on

one who may bring him happiness with children, contentment with age, and perhaps help him to a little fortune in the thatched cottage 'below the elems by the bridge'.

Edward Thomas, *In Pursuit of Spring*
Dorset

THERE WERE SEVERAL characters in our village, and one such was 'Freddie', a crotchety old man disliked by many. In Hoxne he had an allotment which he cared for but neither would he let others see what he was doing nor would he exchange his produce, as was the custom, with his neighbours, which annoyed and upset them. The time came, one April, when his onions should have been showing through the ground, but, instead, all that appeared was a crop of weeds.

'An enemy hath done this!' he was heard to cry out. Indeed, a conspiracy had been afoot to teach him a lesson, though I doubt whether it sank home.

Betty Rutterford, *A Wheelwright of Hoxne*
Suffolk

THE KNELL WAS tolling. Bettesworth explained, 'Poor old Edmund's gone, then.'

'What, Edmund Baxter?'

'Ah, he died last night. I see old David Harris t'other day, an' he told me 'twa'n't possible for 'n to last. He'd bin round there – Edmund sent for 'n 'cause 'twas he's birthday, an' he sent for 'n to come an' 'elp keep it. Twa'n't possible for 'n ever to git up no more: he could see that, he said. Ye see, they'd always been mates together, as ye may say. They was about the same age.'

'How old was he?'

'Seventy-three. And that's what David is. He's in his seventy-third year, He carries it well, don't he? But there, he en't never done no hard work, as ye may say, not to wear hisself out same as Edmund . . . Always a good 'n for work, was Edmund. He used always to get up Sundays jest same as weekdays; it didn't make no difference – about four or five o'clock he was up, feedin' and workin' . . . But there, that was his way: he was *reg*'lar. He had his time for gettin' up an' for gwine to bed too, an' he never altered. When the time come at night, he was up and off . . . But he's gone now, poor old feller. They seems to allow he've put some ha'pence together, too.

They don't *know,* but they thinks so. There's they six houses, ye see ... Well, an' so he *ought,* if you come to that. He never was a wasteful, 'xtravagant kind o' feller. In his food, now, 'twas always wonderfully plain; *good,* ye know, but nothin' flash about it; not this way one day an' that 'nother, but same as gwine to bed – *reg'*lar ... Why, he never got married not afore he was – what now? – fifty, I reckon. An' then he married two sisters.'

Before I could vent my astonishment at this, Bettesworth explained, 'One of 'em first; an' when she died then he took t'other. The vicar, he was down on 'n for that; but Edmund says, "Well, if I didn't marry her, somebody else would."'

'You see,' I began, 'its —'

'Illegal, en't it, sir? ... Well, Edmund didn't care.'

'Well, but the vicar didn't marry 'em?'

'No, *he* wouldn't have no hand in't. But Edmund never cared. He wanted her, an' he had her. I dunno 'ow they *did* git married though.'

George Sturt, *The Bettesworth Book*
Surrey

THERE WERE POOR-HOUSES, I remember – just at the corner turning down to the dairy ... In one of them lived an old man who was found one day rolling on the floor, with a lot of pence and halfpence scattered round him. They asked him what was the matter, and he said he had heard of people rolling in money, and he thought that for once in his life he would do it, to see what it was like.

Thomas Hardy, *The Life of Thomas Hardy*
Dorset

IT IS NOW several years since I first met Caleb Bawcombe, a shepherd of the South Wiltshire Downs, but already old and infirm and past work ... I was at first struck with the singularity of Caleb's appearance, and later by the expression of his eyes. A very tall, big-boned, lean, round-shouldered man, he was uncouth almost to the verge of grotesqueness and walked painfully with the aid of a stick, dragging his shrunken and shortened leg. His head was long and narrow, and his high forehead, long nose, long chin and long, coarse, grey whiskers, worn like a beard on his throat, produced a goat-like effect. This was heightened by the ears and eyes. The big ears

stood out from his head, and owing to a peculiar bend or curl in the membrane at the top they looked at certain angles almost pointed. The hazel eyes were wonderfully clear, but that quality was less remarkable than the unhuman intelligence in them – fawn-like eyes that gazed steadily at you as one might gaze through the window, open back and front, of a house at the landscape beyond.

W. H. Hudson, *A Shepherd's Life*
Wiltshire

BY THE DEATH of Mr John Tomlinson, aged eighty-six, one of the oldest residents of Winsford and an interesting character has been removed. He was one of the old type of church vergers, and from a period extending over forty years filled such a position at the ancient church of St Chad's, Over. His death occurred in a singular manner and was unexpected by all except the old man himself. He actually visited his friends and bade them goodbye, and attended the church on Sunday, stating that he should never go again before they carried him there. On the morning of his death he walked downstairs, shook hands with the members of his family and bid farewell, then again mounted the stairs, and died within a few minutes on the landing.

The Carlisle Patriot, 17 May 1901

COUNTRY OCCUPATIONS AND CRAFTS

This morning I saw some frogspawn which had been brought in from a pond, together with some caddis grubs in their funny little cases of sticks and straws; one grub looked very smart – he had stuck his house all over with bits of bright green rush and water plant.

Edith Holden, *The Country Diary of an Edwardian Lady*

It is in the practical accomplishments of rural life more than anything else that the adaptability of the human species has been best demonstrated. In every case invention has been the child of necessity, and a skill once acquired soon transcended its everyday purpose to become a craft in which pride could – and should – be taken. Every member of the community had his or her place: the smith, the hurdle-maker, the cobbler. The village was largely self-sufficient; agriculture was generally the basis for such prosperity as there was, and all other essential crafts were associated with it. Occasionally there were visitors – journeymen who plied their trade from village to village, and who were eagerly awaited on their appointed day – but mostly rural communities produced what they required for themselves.

Rural craftsmen – wheelwright or saddler, thatcher or plough-maker – had their own skills that had been handed down through generations. Thus there was an apprenticeship that was a family affair, and which therefore guaranteed the preservation of such skills. But, when the need of the community no longer existed, the craft died.

VILLAGES WERE TO a large extent self-contained and most of the needs of the inhabitants were supplied by workers within their own borders or in the nearest town. Many specialized occupations were carried on by men who travelled from village to village, and were eagerly welcomed, as they were the repositories of the gossip of the countryside. This was often the case with the cider-makers, who until a few decades ago made cider for farmers and others, generally at the farms, but sometimes at their own residences. Farmers grew large quantities of apples, which were stored in the barn until the arrival of the cider-maker. The juice was expressed by a solid oak frame five feet in height, with a cross-bar in which were two large iron screws with a wrench, which worked on the press-board loosely fitting into a box. One cider-maker made the drink for the farmers in a large district, the charge being 1s. a sack, and the sender finding a man to run the pulper. When apples were plentiful, this man made from 200 to 300 gallons from his own orchard. The pulp was carefully put into horsehair cloths, before being placed in the press, and the difficulty of procuring these was one of the reasons for the discontinuance of cider-making on the farms. The drink was used in the farmer's own house, but chiefly for the labourers during harvest, a gallon of beer or cider being a fairly moderate daily allowance for a reaper.

W. G. Clarke, *Norfolk and Suffolk*

THE BOOT- AND shoe-makers were a busy folk, for the 'ready-made' had not appeared for sale in the village and almost all the village boots were made to order and to measure. My father told me that before I was born there was a time when cobbler's work made employment for forty men and youths. Very likely they served other smaller places round the village; probably, too, they made the long leathern gaiters worn by thatchers, hedgers and carters.

Many, however, made only heavy boots for work on the land; boots of bark-tanned leather, of ponderous size, the soles hand-stitched and studded with rows on rows of large hobnails. The lace-holes had no brass eyelets and the tongues were stitched to the uppers, which gained them the title and reputation of 'water-tights'. These workshops smelt of cobblers' wax and leather, to which my nose, accustomed to the smell of wood, was sensitive . . .

Each farm labourer had his favourite maker, one who had made his boots for him before – good boots that had withstood the tests of wet and snow, and had been renewed more than once by heeling and soling. To be 'dry-a-foot' was a wise maxim of theirs, and they ordered a new pair well in advance, in the summer, so as to give the leather time to harden before the testing winter set in. Old boots, well-worn, served well for wear at harvest time; the rents between uppers and soles only helped to cool feet that often ached on the sun-burnt stubble.

Everyone looked to harvest earnings for the extra money for new boots for the family. And the boot-maker knew this and worked to it; the many pairs he made in advance (on that understanding) were a very important part of his livelihood. The village feast fell at a lucky time for all concerned – just on the edge of winter, when back money, due on harvest earnings, had been paid. Gladly mixing business with pleasure, they all assembled at the boot-maker's house to supper, where they feasted together to the honour of the boots that he had made.

Walter Rose, *Good Neighbours*
Buckinghamshire

THE ROADS WERE not tarmacked in those days. They were very dusty and very dirty – in summer time a large cart drawn by a horse (well, it was a tank really) would spray water on to the roads to lay the dust. In the winter of course the state of the roads was terrible – they were very muddy indeed. In fact they had crossing sweepers who for a tip (possibly one penny – that's one old penny) would sweep a way across the road, so that you could get across without getting muddy.

Markham Hammerton, *We're the Characters Now*
Cambridgeshire

WE ARE NOT likely again to see men breaking stones. When roads needed to be made or repaired, cartloads of very big stones would be brought from the nearest quarry. In some places this would involve taking loads by horse and cart to the nearest station for conveyance by rail to the district where the stones were needed. In our area there were many stone quarries, so that transport to the roads needing them was an easy matter.

The stones would be put in a large heap, often some six or seven yards in length and five or six feet wide, on the verge by the roadside. The stonebreaker held a large iron-headed hammer in his hand and with this broke the stones. Holding each large piece in position with his left foot he would gradually work through the pile, leaving

a heap of the now smaller stones behind him. These would be dealt with sometimes by another man, sometimes by the same man who, with a much lighter hammer, would reduce them to an even smaller size, ready for use.

As these were laid on the road and levelled out by the steamroller, sand and earth were thrown over and brushed in to fill the small gaps and finally washed in to 'settle' the stones.

These roads were hard and rough, but lasted well; while the rough surface gave a grip to the horses' hooves in frosty weather and also prevented the walker from slipping. On the narrow roads and lanes, many of which have since become bridle-paths, grass has grown over the stones, making a softer, but still firm, tread for man and beast.

Jessie M. Stonham, *Daughter of Wyedean and Kernow*
Herefordshire

BILL TIDY TURNED up on the common one day, and came to our cottage seeking knives to grind or kettles to mend – a real old-time tinker. We found him some work, and soon discovered that he really did grind knives and scissors so that they cut. He was in fact a genuine craftsman and not an artful dodger who had bought a fourpenny file with which to utterly ruin the tools of simple folk who trusted him.

He came at intervals after that first visit and I got on well with him. Formerly he had pushed his 'contrapshun' by hand, but he was getting old and conceived the idea of mounting it on an ancient wagonette so that he could use a pony and drive round the countryside.

It was odd to see him perched high on the vehicle, and his signboard on the front depicting the emblems of his trade was a work of art . . . One spring he failed to turn up. The cold winds of winter had taken their toll.

Reg Gammon, *One Man's Furrow*
Hampshire

THERE WAS A local hurdle-maker . . . I used to see him sometimes in the woods making his wattle hurdles, hay cribs and thatching spars. It seemed an ideal occupation on a warm sunny day to sit thus in the quiet of the woods and weave the rough hazel sticks into such interesting and useful forms. His method was to buy the standing coppice wood and make his goods on the spot. News that he was at work in a certain wood would soon get round and the farmers would go there and make their purchases from the stacks piled up where the living wood had lately

stood, or give orders for any special articles required. Later on a wagon would be sent to bring home the purchases or completed orders.

H. S. Joyce, *I Was Born in the Country*

FATHER WOULD WORK very hard in those days, with only a pushbike to get around on. Few farmers would deliver and fetch their repaired harness, and he had to cycle to them to fetch the harness, including collars and saddles. He had a way of loading his bike with two collars hanging each side from a carrier over the back wheel, and usually a saddle on top and smaller pieces of harness on the handlebars . . . Father had large white leather hides hung up in his shop from which he made hedging cuffs, thongs for the farm carters' boots, and heavy stitching leather for horse collars and saddles etc. For stitching he used large curved needles with a steel palm tool which he pushed the needles in with. The tool was shaped into a tapered solid end about two inches long and three-quarters of an inch in diameter; this had a hole in the end large enough to take his large curved needles, and he used it to pull the needle through. In harvest time, to make a change, Father would sometimes help out a farmer friend with wheat loading and working with a steam-driven threshing machine.

Harold A. Quainton: Mollie Harris, *From Acre End*
Oxfordshire

NOW AND THEN a wagon will appear upon the skyline, and move slowly along the ridge, or a group of gleaners working in the harvest-fields. All the women wear the old-fashioned sunbonnets. Now and then, a year or two ago, a smock-frock might actually have been seen, far and few between indeed, perhaps only two or three remaining in the whole of the valley. Even the oldest men have given them up; 'They have grown too proud,' an old woman said to me rather sadly one day. Her husband had given up wearing his before he died, but she 'did like to see him in it when it was washed and clean'. Being of a frugal mind, and apparently not sharing the pride with which she accredited her husband, she had cut it up and made it into a 'wropper' for herself, and 'a beautiful wropper it had made.'

Strange, when one thinks of it, this discontinuance of the smock-frock. Has the need for it departed, with the decrease of human agricultural labour, and the increase of machinery, or is the reason for its disuse to be found simply in a change of fashion? Is it really, as the old woman in the Lambourne valley said, that the men have grown too proud to wear them, or is it not quite possible that the fault lay partly with the women, who no longer possessed the patience required for making them? The beautiful needlework which went to the fashioning of these old country garments needed plenty of that admirable virtue; the smock-frock was not made in a day. Whatever the reason for its departure, it has gone; and when one visits the picturesque villages that now know it no more, one cannot help regretting its absence. For it would still well fit into the picture.

'L.S.', *Untravelled Berkshire*

MR BUCKINGHAM, A jeweller and clock-mender, he came from Woodstock on a bike … I don't suppose he sold much jewellery in our village, but no doubt he found a few clocks and watches to mend. He also sold wedding rings with a present given for every purchase, and reading spectacles at a shilling a time. There was Mr Wright who pushed a truck about the place selling odds and ends – we used to holler after him, 'Mr Wright, you're not quite right,' and then run away as fast as we could in case he caught us.

Then there was the rag-and-bone man. He had a little truck too that he pushed about and he would give us a penny for a rabbit skin. You could hear him all over the village calling, 'Any rags bones or rabbit skins …' We often had travelling gypsies come round selling clothes pegs and bits of odds and ends. One woman, a Mrs Pratley, came round regular; she'd call at our house and ask, 'Anything out the basket, lady?' There were knots of tape and elastic, bootlaces and clothes pegs that her husband used to make from willow sticks, and soap, two sorts: she'd say to our mother, 'Now ma'am, do you want scented or disinfection?'

Temperance Beatrice Hawtin, née Hanks: Mollie Harris, *From Acre End*
Oxfordshire

IN THE OLDEN days when the cloth trade was flourishing in Berkshire each village was alive with busy industrial enterprise. Each cottage had its spinning-wheel, and every week the clothiers of Reading and Newbury used to send out their men among the villages, their packhorses laden with wool, and every week they returned,

their pack laden with yarn ready for the loom. We give a view of the village of East Hendred, which was a prosperous clothing centre. There is a picturesque field near the church where terraces still remain, which were used for drying cloth, and a piece of land called 'Fulling Mill Meer' where . . . 'ancient people remembered the ruins of a mill in the stream hard by' . . . All this testifies to the importance of this little village in former days, and of the flourishing manufacture of cloth carried on there.

P. H. Ditchfield, *The Charm of the English Village*

IT IS BY no means easy to tie a knot neatly and effectually in straw, and the younger generation of labourers are often impatient of the intractability of the stuff and prefer, when they can, to provide themselves with pieces of twine. Their fathers and mothers, having learnt the old sheaf-knots almost in infancy, tie them with inimitable rapidity and deftness, though they are often unable to do it deliberately or in material other than straw and are nearly always totally incapable of explaining the process in words.

T. Hennell, *Change in the Farm*

THE COMPLETE WHEELWRIGHT, acquiring skill of eyes and hands to make a wheel, was a good enough workman then for the job of building a wagon throughout and painting it too; and all this was expected of him. There was a tale (of another shop than mine) of an aged man who, having built and painted a wagon, set about 'writing' (lettering) the owner's name and address on the small name-board fixed to the off-front side. He managed all right until he came to the address, 'Swafham' or 'Swayle', but this word puzzled him. He scratched his head, at last had to own himself baffled; and appealed to his mate. 'Let's see, Gearge,' he said, 'blest if I ain't forgot how you makes a Sway!'

Gearge showed him.

Truly there were mysteries enough, without the mystery of 'writing', for an unlettered man. Even the mixing and putting on of the paint called for experience. The first two coats, Venetian-red for the underworks and shafts and 'lid colour' (lead colour) for the 'body', prepared the way for the putty, which couldn't be 'knocked-up' by instinct; and then came the last coat, of red-lead for the wheels and Prussian-blue for the body, to make all look smart and showy.

George Sturt, *The Wheelwright's Shop*
Surrey

I WAS BORN in a very picturesque and completely unspoilt village in Northamptonshire where the houses were built of soft, golden-brown stone, a colour that always made you think of sun-baked days – even in winter they seemed to glow with hidden warmth. They were topped with generous, golden straw thatch, done as only thatchers who have had their skills and know-how handed down by their forefathers could, in the traditional Northamptonshire style. Thatching always seemed to run in families and all trade secrets were closely guarded and handed down from father to son. They felt pride in their work (no hurrying by with eyes down and fearing winter storms for them) – indeed, on a Sunday morning they would stand and admire their handiwork. 'We did that,' they would say with pride. They would know each other's work as they travelled through the county and villages around – 'Jim Hartwell did that,' 'Percy Brookes did that,' as sure as if they had signed their names on a board and pinned it to the ridge.

D. A. Judd, *Living in the Country*
Northamptonshire

I COULD HEAR the sound of the woodman's bill-hook and axe felling the straight, eight-year-old chestnut underwood growing higher up the hillside. Standing in the valley I had seen the blue smoke from his wood fire curling up into the crystal clean air, and long before I reached him the scent of wood smoke came to my nostrils.

The countryman will usually talk willingly of his work. For cutting forty-eight walking sticks he is paid sixpence, for twenty-five broomsticks threepence, for twenty-five beansticks threepence, for twenty-four scout-poles fourpence, and so on. His mate was shaving hoops on a 'brake' fixed up underneath a canvas shelter. Every winter for years he has been doing this work – a skilled country trade that is in danger of falling into decay because of the decreasing demand for barrel-hoops. At one time hoops were required in various lengths from two feet to fourteen feet, but now only three or four sizes are wanted, making it difficult to earn a living wage. A bundle of chips is usually allowed to the cutter each day, with a shoulder stick to carry it home. He stacks these in his garden for next winter's fuel, and the odd ends of log-wood are sold to a neighbour, who usually borrows a horse and cart on Saturday afternoon and brings them home.

Reg Gammon, *One Man's Furrow*
Hampshire

PLOUGH SHARES WE made for the old wooden plough. Two anvils were used for this job . . . It was hard work swinging the heavy sledgehammer. One of the first tools I noticed and was taught to use. Soon I had to take the shoes off and finish the hoof and clench up . . . Shoe bumping or making shoes out of old large shoes with half an old shoe. I had to bend the old shoes ready for this job. Men came from London, mostly two together. They used to stay about two days and make shoes and were paid so much a dozen. They were clever and smelt a bit.

Gaius Carley, *The Memoirs of Gaius Carley*
Sussex

THATCHING WAS A separate craft that had not changed, when I first knew of it, in either materials or method. The straw still came from wheat grown in the parish, and was laid on the roofs according to strictly unchanged traditional practices. But the quality of the straw was not so good as formerly, for the threshing machine had damaged it. Old Enoch often said that when corn was threshed by flails a good coat of thatch lasted twenty years, whereas with machine-threshed straw it would only last ten. He also said that to save the straw from being broken by the flails the ears of corn were often chopped off and threshed separately . . . The thatchers worked in pairs, the master on the roof laying the straw in place, and his assistant preparing the yolms and carrying them up the ladder for use. The yolms were small bundles of straws, each straight and in order: the assistant prepared them by pulling handfuls from a pile; the pulling action caused them to be parallel. The thatchers' system was to lay a strip as wide as could be reached to the right side of the ladder, extending from eaves to ridge. This they called a stulch. At both eaves and ridge, also at hips, barges and gables, in fact at any projection of the roof liable to damage by gales, they fastened the thatch down with cleft willow or hazel sprays. These not only secured it, but also gave what seems essential to all craft work – an effective finish.

Walter Rose, *Good Neighbours*
Buckinghamshire

WHEN NOT AT school we watched all that went on. We watched at the forge where the blacksmith had his glowing embers – puffed by bellows – and beat out the iron for the horseshoes. We took our pony to be shod. She stood quietly while the farrier lifted her legs, one by one, between his knees and hammered the nails into the new shoes. She knew they were necessary for the hard roads. The want of a nail might lead to greater mischief later on. Across the road from the farrier, there was the slaughterhouse. We stared, half-frightened, across the wooden fence. The doomed animal was hauled by a rope round its neck to the post – and the pole-axe fell accurately on its forehead – killed by a single blow. On to the corn mill, where corn has been ground for 1,000 years – between the upper and nether millstones. It was worked by the water-wheel. The miller, all white with flour, showed us how it was done, reminding us that:

> *Though the mills of God grind slowly,*
> *Yet they grind exceeding small.*

Sometimes in the hot summer there would be the sound of the fire-bell next door to us. 'Rick afire!' The firemen would come running in, get out the hand-pump, round up and harness the horses and rush off at the gallop. A glorious sight!

Rt. Hon. Lord Denning, *Country Living*
Hampshire

THE STRANGE SMELLS of the smithy attracted me, and I stood as near the open door as I dared. The blacksmith was a morose man, in his leathern apron, dark and torn. His face was dark, his hair coal black, his temper was irritable, he shouted strange oaths, and threw down his hammer with such a clatter it was like doom. He blew up the fire with wheezing bellows, and a shower of golden sparks went through the hole in the roof to the trees above. He shaped the horseshoe on the anvil and the sharp clang of the hammer rang through the marketplace like a bell. I heard it as I sat outside the barber's shop, I heard it when I spent my halfpenny, or when I peered at the druggist's store. It dominated the place, and the pungent smell of burnt hoof and hair and ammonia swept through the doorway. He returned the shoe to the fire, and he carefully pared the hoof, and hammered again at the shoe.

There was something primitive and romantic about a blacksmith, and I remembered our fireside riddle of winter days.

A shoe-maker makes shoes without leather
With all the four elements put together –
Fire, Water, Earth, Air,
And every customer takes two pair.

At school I had learned

Under the spreading chestnut tree
The village smithy stands.

I played 'The Harmonious Blacksmith with variations' for my music teacher. Life was full of blacksmiths. Even the Christmas coloured almanac was a picture of a blacksmith's shop.

In winter the horses were brought down to the village to be sharpened. The heel of the shoe was sharpened and frost nails put in the front. This kept them from slipping on the icy hillsides and glassy roads. To have the horses sharpened was the first sign of bad and dangerous weather, and they were led at walking pace to the smithy.

Alison Uttley, *Country Hoard*
Derbyshire

NEAR THE HEAD of the glen stood an ancient mill, with overshot wheel that hung in its well unhidden by penthouse or roof. Thither a former generation of children had come to stand spellbound watching the resistless sweep of the great floats that brought forth thunder and lightning withal from the seething depths below, flinging the white spray far and wide and bedewing with pearls the mosses and ferns that grew in the chinks of the wall.

Eleanor G. Hayden, *Travels Round Our Village*
Berkshire

CHURCH AND INN

Walked to the Lake of Menteith and back across the hills ... The lake is noted for the number of large pike it contains. The walls of the little inn-parlour on the edge of the lake are hung round with fine, stuffed specimens in cases, that have been captured in its waters.

Edith Holden, *The Country Diary of an Edwardian Lady*

The visitor to most British villages will probably look instinctively for the most abiding local institutions: the church and the pub. There are exceptions: Martin, for example on the Hampshire/Wiltshire border, has no inn, and worshippers in some of the smaller communities frequently had to undertake a journey to church in a nearby village. Usually, however, the two are the pillars of local life, often tolerating one another across a narrow stretch of village green, for there has always been a tension between them. It is interesting that while the Victorian parson preached on the evils of drink, the agricultural labourer was having beer or cider as his staple beverage for refreshment in the fields. At the same time, the image of a pint of frothing ale, together perhaps with a plate of thick-cut bread and cheese on a warm summer's day, is as strong a part of 'dream England' as is the idea of the half-timbered inn with its red-faced avuncular landlord.

The ancient link between church and inn lies as much in music as in anything else. Thomas Hardy's generation had recourse to memories of the 'quire' – who accompanied hymns and psalms in the West Gallery of many a parish church. In his short story, 'Absent-mindedness in a Parish Choir', he tells us of the dire consequences that awaited one group of musicians who forgot where they were, and mistook church pew for village inn party. The Mellstock Quire have their kin in some of the personalities in the following pages . . .

AN IMPORTANT HOUSE in every village is the inn – a hostel such as Izaak Walton loved to sketch, 'an honest alehouse where we shall find a cleanly room, lavender in the windows, and twenty ballads stuck about the wall, where the linen looks white and smells of lavender, and a hostess cleanly, handsome and civil.' Perhaps our village, if it lies along one of the old coaching roads, has more than one such hostelry, and the Blue Lion frowns on the Brown Bull, and the Raven croaks at the Bell. Once they were large and flourishing inns, but their glory has departed. When coaches rattled through the village these inns had a thriving trade, and imagination pictures to our minds the glowing life of the coaching age. We see again the merry coach come in, the 'Mercury', or the 'Regulator', or the 'Lightning', according to the road we chose or the age in which we are pleased to travel. We see the strangely mixed company that hangs about the door, the poor travellers trying to thaw themselves before the blazing hearth, the good cheer that awaits them – huge rounds of beef, monstrous veal pies, mighty hams, and draughts of good old English ale brewed in yon ruined brewhouse, and burgundy and old port.

P. H. Ditchfield, *The Charm of the English Village*

YOU COULD PLAY darts, or six or eight or ten could sit down at the table and have a game of tippet. You put twenty-one strokes on the table – chalk strokes. Whoever won the toss for to hold the coin, you put all ten hands on the table and the others, like, had to guess which hand it's in. They'd say, 'Take he away, take he away, take so-and-so away,' and as you'd win you'd cross out a stroke. You don't see none of those strokes today. 'Tippet' that was called.

We had skittles, see skittles, rings, darts, yes! Rings used to be a hell of a game. You had a board with hooks on it and then you had rubber rings. You used to fling them up and try to put them on the hooks. And of course, later on the cards come on, see, and we would play that. Every Saturday night if you weren't down the pub by half past six you couldn't get in. Because there was about eight high waiting to play and first come first served. You had to wait till they played the game right through and then you were allowed to take on the winners. The losers finished. We used to play for a sixpence.

See, they never had nowhere else to go. There was no club rooms, no village hall, nothing like that in those days, so if they wanted enjoyment they had to go to the pub.

Harry Gillham, *The Nineties*
Dorset

THERE WAS ONE public house in the village and another, which called itself an hotel, opposite the railway station; but the railway station was never looked upon as part of the village as it lay at the extreme end of the houses and was not known even officially by the name of the village. The public house stood exactly opposite the church gate and did a reasonable trade with the villagers in beer and tobacco. Sometimes a shooting or fishing party would call for a bread and cheese lunch. They were always given a little room at the back. No respectable person outside the working class ever entered the bar; it was one of those things that was not done. 'Going into pubs' was not the thing that a man would do who valued the respect of his neighbours. And he did not sneak in the back way so that none might see him. If he wanted a drink he sat on his horse or remained in his gig and the drink was brought out to him; so that any passer could see what he had and how much of it.

H. S. Joyce, *I Was Born in the Country*

It was Christmas week and the tap-room of the Brickmakers' Arms was full. Soon ... the conversation turned to the subject of the season's festivities, and to the jolly times the people used to have on the commons. One or two of the oldest lamented that the old traditional spirit had died out, and that the celebrations of recent years were not so comparable to those of forty or fifty years previous; and this naturally was agreed to by many present. Among the company was Abel Collins, the last surviving member of the Wheeler End Mummers. He took up the discourse and asserted that times were changed for the worse now that mumming with other diversions had ceased.

He said that in his time the young men, on the approach of Christmas, were full of joyous anticipation at the prospect of visiting the neighbouring farms and villages to give the play which had been handed down in the hamlet from time immemorial ... When the conversation had proceeded further, the Mummer was asked whether he could remember the words, and he replied that he thought he was able to do so, although so many years had elapsed since he had taken part in its performance. At this, some of the company pressed him to repeat them, and to their request he willingly consented.

Standing in the centre of the tap-room he went through the whole play without the slightest hesitation, accompanying each character with suitable gestures and actions, to the delight of all assembled.

H. Harman, *Sketches of the Bucks Countryside*

FORDLOW MIGHT BOAST of its church, its school, its annual concert and its quarterly penny reading, but the hamlet did not envy it these amenities, for it had its own social centre, warmer, more human and altogether preferable, in the tap-room of the Wagon and Horses.

There the adult male population gathered every evening, to sip its half-pints, drop by drop, to make them last, and to discuss local events, wrangle over politics or farming methods, or to sing a few songs 'to oblige'.

It was an innocent gathering. None of them got drunk; they had not money enough, even with beer, and good beer, at two pence a pint. Yet the parson preached from the pulpit against it, going so far on one occasion as to call it a den of iniquity. ' 'Tis a great pity he can't come an' see what it's like for his own self,' said one of the older men on the way home from church. 'Pity he can't mind his own business,' retorted a younger one. While one of the ancients put in pacifically, 'Well, 'tis his business, come to think on't. The man's paid to preach, an' he's got to find summat to preach against, stands to reason.'

Flora Thompson, *Lark Rise to Candleford*
Oxfordshire

EVERY LITTLE CHURCH had its band, fiddles and viol, ophicleide and flute. These instrumentalists attended all weddings and other festivals, and at Christmastime trolled out carols in the frosty night air. It is only yesterday since these old village bands died out, and the parish chests still contain their sheets of rudely written music – carols, country dances and old ballads.

Stewart Dick, *The Cottage Homes of England*

MOST O' THE services were took by 'local' preachers, though it depends what you mean by 'local'. They were lay preachers from the other villages round about, but some on 'em come from as far away as eight or nine mile, and ha'nt no way 'o travelling on'y Shanks's pony. One man I knowed walked eight mile or so each way nearly every Sunday to take a service somewhere. The congregation used to take it in turns to have the preacher to tea, and a great occasion it were for the family. The child'en 'ould all be schooled for days aforehand about minding their manners, and then they'd sit round the table scrubbed and washed and not daring to speak while the stranger were there. One poor woman what 'ad come from a better family but 'ad married and had a big family, and 'ad got very poor – gone downhill – used to look for'ard to having the preacher. She'd go to such a lot o' trouble to save and pinch to get a few special things together to eat for the great day. Once when it were 'er turn, she'd got the table all set and the visitor just ready to sit down when one of her older child'en come 'ome unexpectedly and stared at the table and then said, 'What a' yer got a sheet on the table fo' mother?' Poor woman were confused, but the ol' boy didn't know no better. He'd never seen a white tablecloth affore, if 'ed ever seen one at all. The best a lot o' folks had were sacks cut open, made of a sort of grey linen stuff, what the farmers had seed in.

William Henry Edwards: Sybil Marshall, *Fenland Chronicle*
Huntingdonshire

THE CHAPEL STOOD on a small natural plateau roughly in the middle of the village. We were told it was God's house, but we didn't think *He* would have much time to visit our chapel in person.

The chapel was looked after by a couple of the most respected villagers, and was kept clean and polished by Mrs Protheroe.

We knew we had to mind our Ps and Qs in there, but it was a small and friendly house, with no pretensions of grandeur. It did not feel hollow and cold, nor at all overpowering. The windows were of plain glass, and bursts of sunshine brought out extra gleams on the wooden forms polished with such fervour by Mrs Protheroe.

It was quite pleasant to go there on wet Sundays and cold Wednesday evenings. We could still enjoy ourselves, and pass muster with the Sunday school teachers, even with our attention divided between them and our mischief.

The chapel did not have a ghoulish graveyard, either. Our Methodist preachers tried to take care of our souls, but the church, a couple of miles away, had to dispose of our mortal remains.

A simple place, our chapel, yet when the congregation joined together in a full-throated rendering of a favourite hymn, many of us shared a true communion with each other.

The women from the better-off end of the village and a sprinkling of the husbands were regular chapelgoers. Not so the other end. All too often the poorer women 'hadn't a rag on their backs good enough for chapel!'

We were the in-betweens in chapel attendance too, but every so often the love of music in Mam's Welsh blood drew her to chapel on a Sunday evening for the joy of hymn singing.

Winifred Foley, *A Child in the Forest*
Gloucestershire

TIME WHICH BRINGS in its train such changes as parish councils, steam-rollers and other kindred boons, while sparing the fabric of the church, has worked its will upon the interior. Square pews where 'a body med sleep comfe'ble wi'out all the par'sh knawin' on't', have been swept away to make room for more public and less sleep-inducing seats; whitewashed walls have been coloured, ceilings removed, and various other modest ornaments and improvements introduced.

Some of these caused at first grave doubts in the minds of the people: the reredos, erected to conceal a strip of bare wall beneath the east window and sufficiently devoid of artistic merit to have satisfied the most rigorous Protestant, was particularly obnoxious; the characters Alpha and Omega, together with the unobtrusive cross with which it was adorned, being regarded as Popish symbols that had no part nor place in 'our religion'. The substitution of a heating apparatus for stoves with long black chimneys that soared upward to the roof, was also viewed unfavourably, owing

to the predilection pipes are known to entertain for bursting at ill-considered moments. On one occasion they seemed likely to vindicate this view of their character. It was during a severe frost, and the pipes, not having been completely emptied before the cold came on, still contained a small quantity of water. This froze, so that when the warm water began to circulate, the ice gave way with loud cracks like pistol shots, and a fearful joy was to be seen depicted on the faces of the prophets of evil. They 'knawed how 'twud be all along, bless 'ee; a coorse them pipes 'ull bust – pipeses allus do – an' they 'ull blow up theirselves, an' the church, an' iverybody in't.'

Eleanor G. Hayden, *Travels Round Our Village*
Berkshire

By 1884 ALL the children had Sunday clothes. Who shall say how much these added to the set-apart quality of the day? Mothers were showing a degree of that divine, 'amazing love' of which the hymns sang – laundering the little girls' white bonnets of starched and goffered muslin, making them Sunday frocks for summer out of old petticoats of machine-made broderie anglaise, or winter ones from old cloth garments rendered new by blue and scarlet braid. Even the little boys had Sunday coats. It was more difficult to retain a pair of breeches for Sunday, for the little boys felt now that woman-made breeches, with their uncertain outlines, were an indignity, and cried bitterly when their mothers made them.

Was it perhaps the Sunday schools which now had had over sixty years of existence, and one of them more, that had made so holy the Sabbath? The children sat there in the little circular classes of six or ten and heard fascinating stories and modern homely interpretations. There had been a great change in fifteen years; they sang now of 'the lily of siloam' and 'Sharon's dewy rose' and hushed their voices to a whisper to sing of little Samuel in the dark courts of the Temple. Gentle confidence was being instilled, now, into their minds instead of fear of death and punishment:

I think when I read that sweet story of old
When Jesus was here among men
How he called little children as lambs to his fold;
I should like to have been with them then.

Yet some disapproved of the changes. Old labouring women might be seen eyeing the children and grown-ups on their way to church and chapel so washed, shaven and starched. To them this change was trivial. More pigs in the sty, more food on the table, more independence to answer back to farmer and vicar – those were 'proper'. But the labouring life as they had known it was of the earth earthy, and none the worse for that.

M. K. Ashby, *Joseph Ashby of Tysoe*
Warwickshire

THE CHURCH ONCE housed the village school and in the gallery the village orchestra with flute, bassoon, drums and cellos made a joyful noise unto the Lord. Lofty read the psalms from the bottom tier of the pulpit and over the pulpit was a sound board. For eighty-nine years Lofty lived in his thatched black-and-white, wattle-and-daub cottage. Besides making ladders, he made hurdles and gates. He was born in 1858 and his memory was very good. One of his recollections was of an old villager telling the parson he was like the fingerpost: 'He points the way, but never goes there.'

Fred Archer, *Under the Parish Lantern*
Worcestershire

THIS WAYSIDE CHURCH, lost in the featureless plain, was full of oddments, each visualizing some forgotten zeal or activity of the old village life. There was an old oak chest that once contained the copes and other vestments of the priests. Opposite it was a massive tomb, somewhere about 1800, hiding the bones of one Spiers who left annual top-coats and gowns for the needs of the village, and this endowment is still preserved, though now confined to one top-coat and one gown every year. There were several Elizabethan brasses and a fine carved piscina. My guide conducted me from one monument and relic of a once-throbbing life to another and it was as diligently if surreptitiously that I looked at her as at the memorials of the old village craftsmen. Supremely was she the vicar's daughter, the grand archetype of all the legendary daughters of all the legendary vicars and as real to us as dragons, knights and fairy princesses. Her voice 'gentle and low', her courteous manner and wan smile were an evocation of something that had utterly vanished from the world.

H. J. Massingham, *Through the Wilderness*
Wiltshire

IF WE WERE in church early we used to hear Mr Charlie Dustow shout 'Stand' between the peals; and sometimes the six ringers would take so long turning down their sleeves and putting on their coats that, before they had reached the north aisle, Mr Bellamy would be waiting to begin 'When the wicked man turneth away from wickedness which he hath committed, and doeth that which is lawful and right, he shall save his soul alive.' Bert Paddy, a well-knit, square-shouldered figure, used to lurch as he turned into the narrow space between the front seat of the nave and the pulpit. On festival days our hearts would beat for the safety of our decorations.

Ann Treneer, *Cornish Years*

COUNTRY GARDENS AND DOMESTIC LIFE

March 21st. Two thrush's nests with eggs in the garden, in a laurel and an *arbor vitae* bush. Blackbirds building in the holly hedge. Wrens building in the ivy against the house.

Edith Holden, *The Nature Notes of an Edwardian Lady*

Cottages and their gardens belong together because, quite simply, one was an extension of the other. Indoors there remains for us the image of a sometimes spartan existence, but also of white crisp linen, a roaring fire, blackened cottage beams and a table groaning under the weight of simple wholesome food: a seductive picture, brought back to town by professional chroniclers. The fact was usually less romantic; many of the cottages were very old, which perhaps did not have the same charm then as now; and if the man toiled all day in all weathers, then so did the woman of the household, and her work went on long after dark.

To step out into the garden, as the cottager usually did on a summer's evening, was to be met with the picture of a glorious chaos of colour – foxgloves standing against an ancient wall, roses, of course, and also honeysuckle and hollyhocks living amongst a drowsy murmur of bees, (an image reinforced by paintings by Allingham and Quinton). Country gardens were beautiful, but they were also useful; they were living larders – vegetables often grew side by side with flowers – and they were medicine cabinets too, with herbs mixed in among other plants. As ever in the countryside, beauty and practicality walked side by side, hand in hand.

LOOKING BACK ACROSS the years I listen to the summer afternoon cooing of my aunt's white pigeons, and the soft clatter of their wings as they flutter upwards from the lawn at the approach of one of the well-nourished cats. I remember, too, the smell of strawberry jam being made; and Aunt Evelyn with a green bee-veil over her head ... The large rambling garden, with its Irish yews and sloping paths and wind-buffeted rose arches, remains to haunt my sleep. The quince tree which grew beside the little pond was the only quince tree in the world. With a sense of abiding strangeness I see myself looking from an upper window on a confusion of green branches shaken by the summer breeze. In an endless variety of dream-distorted versions the garden persists as the background of my unconscious existence.

Siegfried Sassoon, *Memoirs of a Fox-hunting Man*
Wiltshire

ON LIGHT EVENINGS, after their tea-supper, the men worked for an hour or two in their gardens or on the allotments. They were first-class gardeners and it was their pride to have the earliest and best of the different kinds of vegetables. They were helped in this by good soil and plenty of manure from their pigsties; but good tilling also played its part. They considered keeping the soil constantly stirred about the roots of growing things the secret of success and used the Dutch hoe a good deal for this purpose. The process was called 'tickling'. 'Tickle up old Mother Earth and make her bear!' they would shout to each other across the plots, or salute a busy neighbour in passing with, 'Just tickling her up a bit, Jack?'

The energy they brought to their gardening after a hard day's work in the fields was marvellous. They grudged no effort and seemed never to tire. Often, on moonlight nights in spring, the solitary fork of someone who had not been able to tear himself away would be heard and the scent of his twitch fire smoke would float in at the windows. It was pleasant, too, in summer twilight, perhaps in hot weather when water was scarce, to hear the *swish* of water on parched earth in a garden – water which had been fetched from the brook a quarter of a mile distant. 'It's no good stintin' th' land,' they would say. 'If you wants anything out you've got to put summat in, if 'tis only elbow-grease.'

Flora Thompson, *Lark Rise to Candleford*
Oxfordshire

MY FATHER DIED in 1903 when I was very small, leaving my mother to bring up three children under ten years old. Remarkably for a woman of her generation, she decided to take over as breadwinner and assumed my father's job as a travelling agent to Chappell Pianos. Of course, it was quite unheard of for a woman to be a sales representative at that time but she saw no other way of supporting the family ... As she would be out on the road, touring all over England, Mother settled my elder sister Dorothy in Halifax with Aunt Nellie, one of my father's sisters. My brother Ernest and I were sent to live with her parents at the vicarage in Shelf, in West Yorkshire, then a small, isolated village. I was five years old ... It was at Shelf that I first started drawing. I don't recall exactly when or what, but I do remember sitting up in bed sketching on the blank backs of the illustrations in some of my books, the shiny surface of the paper, and how my pencil squeaked and skidded over it.

For a curious little girl from the town, there were wonderful and unexpected pleasures in discovering all the flowers and their scents. I loved the wild garlic which grew in the steep wood nearby, with a trickle of a stream at the bottom. I also like the feverfew with its yellow-green leaves, strange odour and daisy-like blooms: I have grown it in my gardens ever since, along with London Pride which bordered the laurel-lined drive to the vicarage.

As in many Victorian households, Sunday at Shelf was dedicated to religious observance which cancelled all other activities. Ernest and I were forbidden to play, and the only book we were allowed was a family Bible with grim, steel-engraved illustrations. I would sit on the garden bench for hours in enforced idleness.

Kathleen Hale, *Country Living*

COTTAGERS, THOUGH EXPERT gardeners, are very often puzzled by the foreign names assigned to flowers, especially to roses, which they dearly love, and which are the chief glory of our gardens whether they be large or small. The roses themselves would scarcely know their names when pronounced by our villagers, so strangely transformed and Anglicized are they. Thus the villagers twist Gloire de Dijon into 'Glory to thee John', and the rose named after the great rose-grower, Dean Reynolds Hole, is called 'Reynard's Hole'. General Jacqueminot becomes in popular nomenclature 'General Jack-Me-Not', and the bright crimson Geant des Batailles becomes 'Gent of Battles' ...

The old favourite roses which you find in these gardens are the Sweetbriar, the Cabbage, the York and Lancaster, the Moss, the old White Damask, the double

white, brother of the pretty pink Maiden's Blush . . . The love of the flower is indeed the 'one touch of nature which makes the whole world kin'.

P. H. Ditchfield, *The Charm of the English Village*

MY CHILDHOOD YEARS were spent on a pleasant farm in the cradle of the Hampshire hills. I have many pleasant memories of a lovely English garden, where fruit trees lined the walls and bees hummed above the flower-beds; where raspberries and strawberries grew to perfection, and the scent of thyme and mint and roses filled the air; a garden at the foot of which flowed a chalk stream, where minnows and 'tiddlers' waited, almost asked, to be caught on the crudest of bent pins, and where birds nested in profusion.

Reg Gammon, *One Man's Furrow*

NOT A FLOWER could look constrained, unnaturally smartened, in the garden at Earlham; . . . if one flower-bed was stuck all over with geraniums like a pin-cushion and rimmed with horrible little monsters of fretted, empurpled foliage, the next might be a bower, a boscage, a ramp of sweet peas, a bushy luxuriance of phlox and rosemary. And especially the border against the slow curve of the wall . . . this was a mazy confusion of everything that gleams and glows and exhales a spicery of humming fragrance. Peacock butterflies, brilliant red admirals, fluttered over the blue mist of sea-lavender; a tree of verbena, the lemon-scented herb of which you pull a leaf whenever you pass, branched out close to the immense old trunk of the wistaria; salvia blue and red, bitter-sweet phloxes white and crimson-eyed, the russet and purple trumpets of the lovely creature afflicted with the name of *Salpiglossis*, they all

rejoiced together, rambling and crowding in liberal exuberance. The gardener might wreak his worst will, scheming for a smart patchwork; but the free soul of the garden escaped him and bloomed tumultuously.

Percy Lubbock, *Earlham*
Norfolk

THE GARDEN HAS often a little orchard attached to it, or fruit trees growing amongst the cabbages and potatoes . . . Pear blossom, cherry blossom, make the garden gay and bright, and we trust that no cold winds or late frosts may come to blight the prospect of a good fruit harvest. 'God tempers the wind to the shorn lamb'. and often in the sheltered garden of a cottage the fruit sets and grows and ripens far better than in the more exposed rectory pleasance, and brings grist to the labourer's scanty store . . . Such country customs and the possession of a good garden which will produce vegetables for the whole year for the rustic family, and provide interest and employment in the evenings, and a perpetual delight to the agricultural labourer, make country life far better than the lot of those who have to live in towns.

P. H. Ditchfield, *Rural England*

IN THE GARDEN, small as it was, flowers and vegetables grew together in close companionship, mingled with the wildings which had strayed in to share the fun. They were not refused a home, so white violets grew among the horseradish, and cowslips grew tall under the wall. On the border under the yew tree grew camomile tufts, yellow-green clusters with stiff white flowers like prim little girls, and the pungent smell was refreshing on a hot day.

Alison Uttley, *Country Hoard*
Derbyshire

'IN JULY,' I SAID, quoting Francis Bacon aloud, 'come gilliflowers of all varieties, musk-roses, the lime-tree in blossom, early pears and plums in fruit, jennetings, quodlins. In August come plums of all sorts, pears, apricots, barberries, filberts, musk-melons, monkshoods of all colours.' I paused, and looked to where Father William leaned over the garden hedge. The veteran grunted.

'There ain't never been no melons in this parish,' he said defiantly; 'man an' boy, I've worked hereby 'ighty year, an' no mistake.'

'I'm telling you what Francis Bacon writes,' I replied.

'Then he's a liar, beggin' y'r pardon,' said Father William irritably. 'I'm an older man nor 'e an' 'e can't teach me.'

'He has been dead three centuries and more,' I said in extenuation.

'Well, well!' remarked the ancient one; 'maybe there was melons in this 'undred then. But there ain't now, not for no Bacon.'

S. L. Bensusan, *A Countryside Chronicle*
Essex

IN THE GARDEN the flowers were homely as the wild ones. They were called by village names. Gillyvers, striped red and yellow, grew under the mossy wall, and golden stonecrops and saxifrages cushioned the wall crannies above them. On the field side were Kexies and the white flowers of Queen Anne's Lace, and tall foxgloves leaned over the top. High on an old roof were cushions of house-leek, with fine tall blossoms. Underneath curled honeysuckle, waving its yellow fingers, like its wild brother across the lane.

Below, in a flower bed was Minnie Net, a sturdy little girl who carried green bags of seeds, not unlike my own gathered hanging-pocket. It was perhaps a workbag to hold scissors and thimble for little Minnie Net. She was a person of character, with perfume in her pockets, and we took a great interest in her stay with us each summer.

Rosy Dandrum was another, but she was a proud flower, sitting erect on a bush, wearing petals woven in one piece without seam. We could slip her dress over her head and leave her naked in her little frills. The purple dress made an excellent hat for a doll. These little mauve Rosy Dandrums were the only ones I saw, and they may have been half wild, for they were very old.

Next came Sweet William, a youth in striped trousers, red and white, or in dark crimson jacket. He was a favourite flower of the village children, who carried him in tight bunches to the school teacher. There was rivalry between the variegated flowers, each child trying to bring the loveliest colours. Sweet William was a male, and I associated him with the Williams I knew – Uncle William, my father's eldest brother, and Young Will our servant boy.

There was Sweet Nancy, a simple little creature in full white skirts, and Pheasant's Eye, staring at us with a look we knew very well in the full-plumed cock-pheasant, and Poppy, holding out her coloured cup of transparent crinkled petals to catch the sunshine. On the border under the gooseberry bushes were Bachelor's Buttons, crimson and white round buttons to sew on somebody's coat, and grey-green Lad's

Love, aromatic and delicious, which the young women slyly inserted in their bunches of flowers. There were giant sunflowers, always turning their broad country faces towards the sun god, and little pansies, which my mother called Love-in-idleness, in many-coloured frocks, close together like a class of children, eager to talk and to see all that was going on. There were Snapdragons, with closed lips ready to open and speak a silent word if one pressed them, and lilies-of-the-valley, with their ivory peals of bells which surely rang when nobody was about. They were the sisters of the wild lilies in the woods.

Alison Uttley, *Country Hoard*
Derbyshire

SHE HAD BEEN in that garden before, but never in May, with the apple blossom out and the wallflowers filling the air with their fragrance. Narrow paths between high, built-up banks supporting flower borders, crowded with jonquils, auriculas, forget-me-nots and other spring flowers, led to the earth closet in its bower of nut trees halfway down the garden, another to the vegetable garden and on to the rough grass plot before the beehives. Between each section were thick groves of bushes with ferns and capers and Solomon's seal, so closed in that in the long, rough grass there was always damp. Wasted ground, a good gardener might have said, but delightful in its cool, green shadiness.

Nearer the house was a portion given up entirely to flowers, not growing in beds or borders, but crammed together in an irregular square, where they bloomed in half-wild profusion. There were rose bushes there and lavender and rosemary and a bush apple tree which bore little red and yellow streaked apples in later summer, and Michaelmas daisies and red-hot pokers and old-fashioned pompom dahlias in autumn and peonies and pinks already budding.

Flora Thompson, *Lark Rise to Candleford*
Oxfordshire

THE LOVE OF flowers is so universal, and the garden may be such a useful adjunct to the cottage, yet there is very great ignorance of the right principles of gardening, and the parson may be of great use to his poorer neighbours, not only by teaching, but still more by showing them better ways in his own garden. For the parsonage garden gate should always be open, and every parishioner welcomed; there need be no fear of any undue advantage being taken of the free permission to enter – the one difficulty will be to induce them to come in. And the parson may do much to brighten the gardens of his parish, and so to increase the interest in them by giving plants from his own garden. I have for many years been a cultivator of hardy plants, and have been able to gather together a large number of species; and I was long ago taught, and have always held, that it is impossible to get or keep a large collection except by constant liberality of giving.

Canon Henry Ellacombe, *In a Gloucestershire Garden*

AT THE BEGINNING of each season Grandfather sat by the fire with a collection of seed catalogues and worked through them, marking everything he thought he'd like to grow . . . Along the borders, each side of the rubble path, he put the bedding plants. He liked showy ones which grew easily and filled the garden with scent and colour. He chose pansies, violas, petunias, night-scented stock, marigolds and asters; at the back of these he had gladioli, Canterbury bells, love-lies-bleeding, lupins and phlox. In the late summer there were great clumps of dahlias and Michaelmas daisies.

All through the season there were roses. He found space for them everywhere. There were ordinary ones, the sweet-smelling kind, with the big, cabbage-fat blossoms, smoking with colour. He named the different varieties with authority,

Madame Plain, Grace Darling, Mrs Herbert Stevens, Melody and Shower of Gold. There were also ramblers, trained against the cottage, over archways and along rustic trelliswork. There were pale pink single ones which smelled sweet and fell apart at a touch. There were those that hung in clusters like minute powder-puffs, and the big, dark pink, single ones with petals spread wide like butterfly wings in the sunshine.

Mavis Budd, *Fit for a Duchess*
Hampshire

THE RECTORY COTTAGES, a very ancient building, filled the west side of the yard . . . There was a tiny knot garden beneath the windows, fenced from the school yard by a low stone wall and patterned out in little formal flower-beds neatly hedged with box. Some steps ascended from this plot to the Rectory garden, bounded on one side by the churchyard wall and shielded to the northward by a row of pollarded elms. The garden was prolific, with a rich, warm soil . . . A myrtle, grown from a sprig . . . stood in the open centre of the garden, six feet high and flowering profusely every year.

Lilian Bond, *Tyneham: A Lost Heritage*
Dorset

EVERY COTTAGER TAKES a pride in his garden, for the flower shows which are held every year result in keen competition. A prize is always given for the prettiest garden among all the cottagers. This is an excellent plan; it brightens and beautifies the village street for eight months in the year. In May the rich brown and gold of the gillyflower is seen on every side, and their fragrance is wafted far and wide by every breeze that blows.

Then there is a very pretty plant that covers some of the cottage walls at this time of year. It is the wistaria; in the distance you might take it for lilac, for the colours are almost identical.

Then come the roses – the beautiful June roses – the *Nimium breves flores* of Horace. But the roses of the Cotswolds are not so short-lived for all that Horace has sung: you may see them in the cottage gardens from the end of May until Christmas.

J. Arthur Gibbs, *A Cotswold Village*
Gloucestershire

THERE IS SOMETHING indescribably cosy about a thatched roof. It seems to wrap a house round like a blanket, and speaks convincingly of warmth and comfort. It softens out all the angularities from the roof-lines, smooths them over with the gentle curves of a snow drift; the dormer windows become little peep-holes like birds' nests, and the overhanging eaves are full of sparrows. And this appearance of snugness is no deception. To one accustomed to the old thatch, a slate or even tile roof is a change for the worse, colder in winter and hotter in summer, for the thatch, like a thick, shaggy hide, is a good non-conductor, and keeps out equally heat and cold.

Stewart Dick, *The Cottage Homes of England*

I AM SORRY to have to record that many old and formerly favourite flowers have vanished from village gardens of today. The vicissitudes of fashion in floriculture remind me of those primitive weather-gauges which in my childhood used to adorn every cottage interior. They were made of grey crusted cardboard, and shaped to represent a Gothic perch, from which emerged when the sun shone, a female figure in bonnet and shawl; the gentleman with old-world chivalry that would, I fear, be little appreciated in these days of athletic women, reserving the bad weather for his own walks abroad. Thus when annuals were 'in' at the Hall, they were 'out' in the village, and cottagers grew such flowers as Sweet William, London Pride, Aaron's rod and the like. Now that all self-respecting upper-class gardens boast a herbaceous border, their humble friends flaunt in the gay colours of begonias, nasturtiums, China asters and stocks. Lilacs, sweet lavender which is never out of date, gillyflowers and tall white Madonna lilies still shed their fragrance through the village; though these are but lightly esteemed compared with annuals and tubers.

Eleanor G. Hayden, *Travels Round Our Village*
Berkshire

WE HAD NONE of those contrivances which are regarded now as essential. No electricity. No telephone. No running water. No toilet or bathroom. Only washbasins and chamberpots.

Look with your mind's eye at the house where I was born. It was 400 years old, built of oak beams filled in with wattle and daub. The kitchen range was fired by coal. All our water was drawn from the well. Each day presented 'the trivial round, the common task'. Pump up the water. Fill the buckets and kettles. Get in the wood and the coal. See to the oil lamp. Make ready the candlesticks. Clean out the stable. Groom the pony. Go to the WC. It was outside at the end of the garden. The night-cart cleared it once a month.

But we were happy for all that. Our forerunners had lived in this way for centuries.

Rt. Hon. Lord Denning, *Country Living*
Hampshire

I LIVED IN a cottage which is still there – four rooms and a very long larder with a brick floor where Mum kept vegetables and a big crock where apples were cut up and soaked for home-made cider. The kitchen had a beam across the ceiling with a big hook where a pig was hung after it had been killed and scraped, a copper which always smoked so that the door had to be left open even in the winter to let out the smoke (it was many years before anyone looked to see what the trouble was and found a brick had lodged in the chimney). There was an open fireplace with a white chalked hearthstone, which had to be cleaned every day with chalk which was brought from the downs . . .

In the front room, as we used to call it, there was coconut matting on the floor which we as children had to take into the orchard every Saturday and pull over the grass to clean it; once the floor was swept and washed it was brought in again. We had a special mantelpiece in the front room with red glasses on, which we were never allowed to touch, but as a treat Mum would gently let them touch each other and make them ring . . .

I remember waking up in the winter to the sound of Mum stirring the porridge with an iron spoon in a big oval iron saucepan. And I remember the same iron saucepan being used on Sunday for an enormous meat pudding, and (being Sunday) Mum in a clean white apron, the big ones with a bib. On Sundays everything sparkled: the knives had been cleaned on the emery board, forks and spoons with

Brasso and the steel on the grate done with emery paper. Mum had been cooking all the morning, and always prided herself that whoever dropped in at teatime had something to eat and a cup of tea. I have known as many as eighteen to come in and Mum had given them all a cup of tea with only half a pint of milk.

Winifred Janes, *Country Living*
Sussex

SOME DALESMEN'S HOUSES have the dwelling-house, barn and stables or cowhouse all under one roof. In the centre is the barn or threshing-floor, with a large pair of folding doors at one end and a small winnowing door at the other. On one side is the dwelling-house, and on the other the stables or ox-house. Sometimes the central part was a sort of passage with doors leading on one side to the habitation of the family, and the other to that of the animals, together with a barn. The reason why we call the entrance to a house the threshold is because the threshing-floor was placed there. In the dalesman's house he used to feed not only his family, but his labourers, who arranged themselves according to seniority at a long table remote from the fire, while he and his family sat at a round table near the hearth.

P. H. Ditchfield, *Rural England*

I CAME TO a long, low farmhouse kitchen, smelling of bacon and herbs and burning sycamore and ash. A gun, a blunderbuss, a pair of silver spurs and a golden spray of last year's corn hung over the high mantelpiece and its many brass candlesticks; and beneath was an open fireplace and a perpetual red fire, and two teapots warming, for they had tea for breakfast, tea for dinner, tea for tea, tea for supper, and tea between. The floor was of sanded slate flags, and on them a long many-legged table, an oak settle, a table piano and some Chippendale chairs. There were also two tall clocks; and they were the most human clocks I ever met, for they ticked with effort and uneasiness: they seemed to think and sorrow over time, as if they caused it, and did not go on thoughtlessly or impudently like most clocks, which are insufferable; they found the hours troublesome and did not twitter mechanically over them; and at midnight the twelve strokes always nearly ruined them, so great was the effort. On the wall were a large portrait of Spurgeon, several sets of verses printed and framed in memory of dead members of the family, an allegorical tree watered by the devil, and photographs of a bard and of Mr Lloyd George. There were about fifty well-used books near the fire, and two or three men smoking, and one man reading some serious book aloud, by the only lamp; and a white girl was carrying out the week's baking, of large loaves, flat fruit tarts of blackberry, apple and whinberry, plain golden cakes, soft currant biscuits and curled oat cakes. And outside, the noises of a west wind and a flooded stream, the whimper of an otter and the long, slow laugh of an owl; and always silent, but never forgotten, the restless, towering outline of a mountain.

Edward Thomas, *Wales*

AN OLD OAK table, with legs as thick and black as those of an elephant, was spread in the homely house-place for the farmer and his family, wife, children, servants, males and female; and heaped with the rude plenty of beans and bacon, beef and cabbage, fried potatoes and bacon, huge puddings, a table where bread and cheese and beer, and good milk porridge and oatmeal porridge were eaten.

Eldred F. Walker, *Bath & West Society*

THE WORKING CLOTHES were corduroys, subdued by long use to the colour of the earth, though rarely they were washed to a creamy whiteness that seemed unnatural. The men's trousers were strapped, or tied with string, under the knees; this, they said, kept in the warmth above and also gave freedom to kneel, or stoop, at work. For work during dirty weather, or for hedging and ditching and such-like rough tasks, long leathern gaiters, buttoned from the ankle to the hips, were worn.

They wore hard, heavy boots, the clean weight of them often doubled by the soil that clung to them while following the plough, so that each step taken over the furrows demanded a sustained upward pull; the ploughman and the boy who led the horses were well known by their manner of walking – a to-and-fro, sideways sway of the head and shoulders down to the pit of the stomach – a gait of which they could not rid themselves even when walking on hard roads.

Walter Rose, *Good Neighbours*
Buckinghamshire

IT WAS A pleasant sight; snowy white cloth, gleaming silver, pink and white tea service, and the food looked so good. There was stiff shiny pork cheese, a plate of pink and white ham, cut very thinly and decorated with parsley; a glass dish of pickled white herrings, also adorned with parsley; a damson cheese, flanked by a jug of thick cream; a dish of rich brown gingerbread, two plates of home-baked bread and butter, stewed pears and custard – a lovely tea.

Mathena Blomefield, *Nuts in the Rookery*

EVEN WITHIN RECENT years, now and then a servant-girl upon entering service at the farmhouse would refuse to touch butcher's meat. She had never tasted anything but bacon at home, and could only be persuaded to eat fresh meat with difficulty, being afraid she should not like it. One girl who came from a lonely cottage in a distant 'coombe-bottom' of the Downs was observed never to write home or attempt to communicate with her parents. She said it was of no use; no postman came near, and the letters they wrote or the letters written to them never reached their destination . . . They sometimes had lettuce pudding for dinner, and thought nothing of eating raw bacon . . . Yet even in far-away coombe-bottom they knew enough to put an oyster-shell in the kettle to prevent incrustation.

Richard Jefferies, *Hamlet Folk*
Wiltshire

WHEN MY FATHER was a young lad in the early part of this century . . . scrounging from the fields and hedgerows was a necessity for poor families in the country. Not only were Mother Nature's products raided with great intensity but any crops grown by the farmers that were fit for human consumption disappeared from the fields in quite large quantities and mysteriously reappeared in back houses and kitchens all over the village. Dad proudly admitted that he was involved in such activities and being a modest sort of a person reckoned that he was one of the best. He apparently poached his first rabbit when he was eight so perhaps his boast was not unjustified.

Bonny Sartin, *A Little Bit of Dorset*

LIFE WITHOUT A pig was almost unthinkable. To have a sty in the garden, or, as often, abutting on the cottage, was held to be as essential to the happiness of a newly married couple as a living-room or a bedroom. So much was the pig a part of domestic life that no vision was satisfactory that did not include the flitch of bacon on the wall of the living-room, and hams and gammons hanging from the ceiling.

The more substantial cottager, midway between the labourer and farmer, kept his breeding sow, and a happy man he was when it responded to wise pre-arrangements and farrowed in the early spring. The news that a litter of (say) ten or twelve sucklings had arrived in the night never failed to create a sensation in the placid life of the village. Cautious peeps over the rude sty fence were allowed, for a glimpse of the happy mother lying flatwise on a bed of clean straw, her sleek black youngsters sleeping, or, as often, securing a teat of luscious milk.

Walter Rose, *Good Neighbours*
Buckinghamshire

THE COTTAGE WHERE we lived was typical of its kind. There was, chiefly, a scullery, kitchen sometimes a parlour or sitting-room and a pantry with a raised brick shelf for salting a pig on. The upstairs accommodation comprised either two or three bedrooms. The scullery had a large copper in one corner. This was heated by a coal fire underneath it. The first task on a Monday morning was to get the fire lit and some water heated for the weekly wash. The other items needed on washday were a wash tub, a mangle and a dolly-tub complete with doll pegs. It was almost a day-long task as many of the clothes had to be starched and some rinsed in blued water;

this treatment made them whiter. The kitchen was fitted with a cast-iron range. The oven sat on one side of the fire and the boiler for heating the water on the other. There were a few different types of ranges but the principle was the same. My father prepared his fire-lighting material each weekend. He made up a bundle of different sizes of sticks for each day of the week. Arising between 5.30 and 6.00 a.m. he would clear out the ashes from the previous day, put some paper in the bottom of the grate, then lay the sticks, small ones at the bottom and the larger pieces at the top. Next he placed the filled kettle on the top of the sticks and put pieces of coal round the kettle and lit the paper. By this time the kettle was boiling and the coal burning but all the sticks had gone. When the kettle was removed the fire was going well and the breakfast was ready. Some women hung a short metal shelf on the bars of the grate; this enabled them to put a flat iron near the fire. When the iron was hot enough, tested by dabbing a wet finger on the iron, another iron was put to the heat and in this way the ironing was done. My mother used to put her irons in the hot oven; she said the face of the iron kept much smoother this way.

G. Cottingham, *To be a Farmer's Boy*
Lincolnshire

PEOPLE MADE UP their own mixtures and medicines. In the house when we had a cold, my mother would bake something that was called a wurzel, a vegetable that was given to the animals like a swede or turnip, that was cut up with brown sugar and baked in the oven, and the juice of that you had. When you had a very bad cold, they had beer in a glass – I suppose it was stout – and they put a poker in the fire, got it hot and plunged it into the beer. Then they put ginger in it and you drank that. We didn't like it very much, but we thought it was a marvellous treat. Also every Friday night every child was given a dose of liquorice powder or Epsom salts. Every child had to have that on Friday because you were not going to school the next day or Sunday school.

Charlotte Huggett, *The Nineties*
Kent

IT WAS ONE of those cottage rooms that contain a wide open fireplace left in its original state; but the dog-irons had given place to a kitchen range backed close to the wall, and the spacious chimney was almost blocked by a large piece of tin placed on the riddy-pole from which the pot hooks and hanger still hung, yet leaving sufficient vent for the smoke to freely ascend. As in most old cottages, the ceiling was low and supported by a transverse beam, the long mantelshelf was crowded with old china and various ornaments of a bygone generation, and on the opposite wall ticked an old-fashioned clock which ... had gone without repairs for close on forty years. Comfortable and inviting the atmosphere was as I sat in the warmth and glow of the fire on that cold dark evening.

H. Harman, *Sketches of the Bucks Countryside*

WASHING DAY LASTED all day; the water had to be carried from the pump and heated in the boiler, then the clothes were washed, then boiled, then steamed, next they were put in a bath of cold water with Reckitts Blue. The only soap was Hudson's Powder and soda was also used. It was real hard work. The old wooden roller mangle was kept outside the door as it was too big to come inside. I can still recall having to stand out there on a bitter cold day and get all that washing through that old wringer.

Mrs Rowe, *Somerset Remembers*

THE TABLE SEATED twelve at Christmas; at other times it was the writing, sewing, cooking table etc. The oven was heated by coal and at Christmas Grandma would sit by the fire putting on one bit of coal at a time so that it got neither too hot or too cold but kept an even temperature for the cakes. There were kitchen chairs under the window with scented geraniums on the sill. There was a small table in the corner where the washing-up was done. Two wooden armchairs – well padded, a bureau, a bookcase, a picture painted on glass...

There was a passageway with a soft water tank, a brick copper, a mangle and – such luxury – an indoor tap and drain. Beyond this was another room, just stone cobbles on the floor, a pump and for summer cooking, a ripingill. We had one of these for years – such a boon. You could have two veg. cooking on the top and something simmering and two things in the oven every day...

The buildings went on two sides of a gravel yard with some flower-beds, a hen run. The hens were fed on scraps from the table with a little corn. There was a brick outplace with the 'loo' at the back. This had a wooden seat with two holes and was emptied from outside. This was not a matter talked about...

Grace Meeks, *We're the Characters Now*
Cambridgeshire

SOME OF THE cottages had two bedrooms, others only one, in which case it had to be divided by a screen or curtain to accommodate parents and children. Often the big boys of a family slept downstairs, or were put out to sleep in the second bedroom of an elderly couple whose own children were out in the world. Except at holiday times, there were no big girls to provide for, as they were all out in service. Still, it was often a tight fit, for children swarmed, eight, ten or even more in some families, and although they were seldom all at home together, the eldest often being married before the youngest was born, beds and shakedowns were often so closely packed that the inmates had to climb over one bed to get into another.

Flora Thompson, *Lark Rise to Candleford*
Oxfordshire

A man's work is from sun to sun
But a woman's work is never done.

That's a rhyme I heard a-many a time when I was young, and as far as the women in the fen, like my mother, was concerned, there's no doubt it were a true saying. If life were hard for the men, it were harder still for the women. They often worked side by side with their menfolk in the fields all day, then went home and whilst their husbands fed the pig or fetched a yoke o' water, they'd get the meal going. But most men could rest a little while after their tea, at least in winter, but the mother had to set about preparing for the next day, getting the children washed and off to bed, and making and mending clothes and what bits o' furniture they had in the house. Then they'd have to be up with the lark in the morning to sweep and clean the house afore it were time to go to work again. Of course not all the women worked all the time, but most of 'em worked on the land in the busy times, and some of em' boasted about being able to do as much as a man at some jobs. There were a lot of jobs a woman's quick neat fingers could do better than a man's, but I d'n't like to see a woman gault-digging, though I have seen 'em a good many times and a lot o' women 'set off' the turf for their husbands in the turf fen.

Then they would always either be carrying a child, or else had just had a new baby, and very often they would have two or three that coul'n't walk. They boasted about the size o' their families, and would be ever so proud so to say they'd got seven or eight sons and four or five daughters. Feeding a family like that on ten shillings a week, which was what the father 'ould bring home, were a job in itself. The money had to cover food and firing and Dad's baccy, but it was mostly what the mother earned that bought clothes and anything else they had to have.

Kate Mary Edwards: Sybil Marshall, *Fenland Chronicle*
Huntingdonshire

THE SIGHT OF these simple pieces of mechanism – mechanism that supplemented but did not supplant hand labour – makes one think how much fuller and more interesting was the rural home life of the older days, when nearly everything for daily use and daily food was made and produced on the farm or in the immediate district; when people found their joy in life at home, instead of frittering away half their time in looking for it somewhere else; when they honoured their own state of life by making the best of it within its own good limits, instead of tormenting themselves with a restless striving to be, or at any rate appear to be, something that they are not. Surely that older life was better and happier and more fruitful, and even, I venture to assume, much fuller of sane and wholesome daily interests. Surely it is more interesting, and the thing when made of a more vital value, when it is made at home from the very beginning, than when it is bought in a shop.

Look at the little silk-winder. Perhaps it belonged, a hundred years ago, to some squire's wife or daughter. She was possibly doing a piece of that pretty old work where a soft narrow silk ribbon is gathered up into little flowers. She wanted some yards of ribbon of a golden colour, something like oat-straw. Nothing of the kind was to be had in the market-town, and she had seen nobody of late likely to be going to London, who could do her commission. So she kept some silk-worms, and when they had done their work she wound off the silken thread from the cocoons on this little winder – a few cocoons at a time bobbing about in a basin of lukewarm water. Then she would wind it off from the dainty hank that had gathered round the pegs of the extended arms, on to the little spools, till she had enough on them to form the threads of the warp and a reserve for the tiny shuttle. And then she had a little loom, home-made – I made one myself once – and wove her golden ribbon.

Gertrude Jekyll, *Old West Surrey*

ACKNOWLEDGEMENTS

There are many people to thank for this book's existence. Fred Archer kindly allowed me to quote from *Under the Parish Lantern* (Hodder & Stoughton), and Mavis Budd permitted me to use extracts from her book, *Fit for a Duchess* (J.M. Dent), as did John Burnett, editor of *Useful Toil* (Routledge). Passages from *A Sussex Life*, edited by Dave Arthur and *Small Talk* by Naomi Mitchison are included with the permission of Barrie & Jenkins and The Bodley Head respectively. I am grateful for permission to reproduce extracts from *The Nineties* by Gloria Wood and Paul Thompson (BBC Books). In quoting from *We're the Characters Now* I acknowledge permission given by the copyright holder, the Workers Educational Association (Chatteris Branch), the editor Susan Oosthuizen and the publisher, Cambridgeshire Libraries Publications. Cambridge University Press granted permission to quote from *Joseph Ashby of Tysoe* by M.K. Ashby, *Fenland Chronicle* by Sybil Marshall and *Good Neighbours* by Walter Rose, and passages from *Cornish Years* by Anne Treneer are reproduced by permission of Jonathan Cape. I acknowledge permission from Myfanwy Thomas and Carcanet Press in quoting from the writings of Helen Thomas in *Under Storm's Wing*. Chatto & Windus published *From Acre End* by Mollie Harris. The recollections of the late Sir Peter Scott came from Jane Longmore's *When I was a Child* (Crocodile Books), reproduced by permission of the Children's Society. Dame Barbara Cartland kindly gave her permission to use part of her piece about a childhood Christmas in *Country Living* magazine, as did Kathleen Hale. My thanks to *Country Living* also for permission to quote from other articles in their 'Country Childhood' column by Lord Denning, Alan Bloom, Winifred Janes and Mollie Keane. *A Wheelwright of Hoxne* by Betty Rutterford was published in 1973 by Terence Dalton Ltd. My thanks to David Burnett at Dovecote Press for permission to quote from *Tyneham* by Lilian Bond, published in 1984. I must thank Faber & Faber and the Alison Uttley Literary Property Trust for permission to quote from *Country Hoard* (1942); *Country World: Memories of Childhood* (1984); and *The Country Child* (1931). I am also grateful to Faber & Faber for allowing me to quote extracts from *Farming Memoirs of a West Country Yeoman* by S.G. Kendall and *Memoirs of a Fox-Hunting Man* by Siegfried Sassoon. Reg Gammon granted permission to quote from his *One Man's Furrow*, published by Webb & Bower, and shared with me a fascinating correspondence in the process. In including extracts from *The Peveril Papers* by Flora Thompson, I acknowledge the Estate of the author, and the publishers, Hutchinson. Quotations from *The Way of a Countryman* and *A Countryman's Creed* by Sir William Beach Thomas are reproduced by permission of Michael Joseph. Judd Publishing and Denis Judd granted me permission to quote from his 1991 book, *Living in the Country*; and likewise Penelope Massingham, to quote from *Through the Wilderness* by her husband, H.J. Massingham. G.K. Nelson was also kind enough to let me select from his 1991 book, *To be a Farmer's Boy* (Alan Sutton). Extracts from *Larkrise to Candleford* by Flora Thompson (1945) are reproduced by permission of Oxford University Press. I thank also A.L. Rowse for extracts from *A Cornish Childhood* published by Jonathan Cape Ltd (1942). My good friend Bonny Sartin of The Yetties kindly let me use extracts from *A Little Bit of Dorset*. I am grateful to the Somerset Federation of Women's Institutes for permission to use copyright material from *Somerset Remembers* (1978). Passages from *Horse and Cart Days* are included by permission of the Executors of the late A.B. Tinsley and the publisher, Clark & Howard Books. In addition there are a number of people who have been generous with their help, advice and time during the making of this anthology; my sincere thanks go to Richard Emeny, Frank Henry, Sybil Marshall, Timothy Rogers, Deputy Keeper of Western Manuscripts at the Bodleian Library, Myfanwy Thomas and Richard Webb. I have endeavoured to contact the copyright holders of all the material included in *A Remembered Land* and apologize to any I have been unable to trace. Finally I thank the spirit of Edith Holden, the inspirer of the book; I hope she would have liked it.

The editor and publisher are grateful to the following for permission to reproduce photographs in this book:
Dorset County Museum (Hardy Collection): photographs on pages: 19, 92, 107, 114, 155; Rural History Centre, University of Reading: 1, 5, 8, 15, 22, 25, 32, 34, 35, 44, 50, 53, 56, 57, 60, 61, 63, 64, 73, 83, 98, 108, 110, 117, 121, 123, 145; Mrs Iris Moon: 75, 94.

Photographs on the following pages are the copyright of the Beaford Archive, Devon: 11, 26, 39, 40, 42, 43, 46 (outdoor concert), 47, 51, 54, 58, 59, 66, 70, 86, 102, 103 (Sunday school outing), 104 (gypsy wedding), 113 (district council resurfacing road), 118, 124, 126, 127, 130 (recast bells being rehung), 136, 138, 142, 143 (school gardening class), 147, 150 and 153 (wearing a special apron for nursing a cat).